HUMAN INFANTS

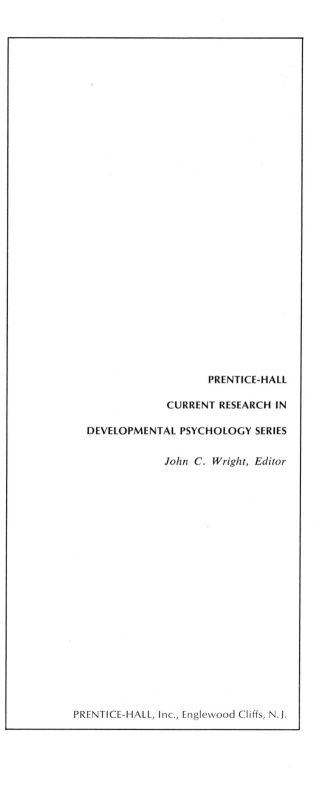

PRENTICE-HALL

CURRENT RESEARCH IN

DEVELOPMENTAL PSYCHOLOGY SERIES

John C. Wright, Editor

PRENTICE-HALL, Inc., Englewood Cliffs, N.J.

HUMAN INFANTS

EXPERIENCE
AND
PSYCHOLOGICAL
DEVELOPMENT

BURTON L. WHITE

Laboratory of Human Development
HARVARD UNIVERSITY

to Jean Piaget

13-445148-1

Library of Congress Catalog Card Number: 75-132911
Printed in the United States of America

Current printing (last digit):
10 9 8 7 6 5 4 3 2 1

PRENTICE-HALL INTERNATIONAL, INC., London
PRENTICE-HALL OF AUSTRALIA, PTY. LTD., Sydney
PRENTICE-HALL OF CANADA, LTD., Toronto
PRENTICE-HALL OF INDIA PRIVATE LIMITED, New Delhi
PRENTICE-HALL OF JAPAN, INC., Tokyo

THE PRENTICE-HALL SERIES
IN DEVELOPMENTAL PSYCHOLOGY

JOHN C. WRIGHT, Editor

PRENTICE-HALL
CURRENT RESEARCH IN
DEVELOPMENTAL PSYCHOLOGY SERIES

JOHN C. WRIGHT, Editor

THE ACQUISITION AND DEVELOPMENT OF LANGUAGE
Paula Menyuk

HUMAN INFANTS:
EXPERIENCE AND PSYCHOLOGICAL DEVELOPMENT
Burton L. White

CONTENTS

4

5

7

My hope is that this little book will be different. I firmly believe that I have a message, and that it is worth delivering. In this, of course, I may be very wrong, but I have promised myself I would try. I am of the opinion that the issue with which I concern myself professionally is extremely important. That issue is "how one might rear a young human so he may most fully realize the potential with which he comes into the world." I have been advised against admitting this interest in public, lest my qualifications as a dispassionate scientist become suspect. Let them be suspect.

This book will not provide the definitive information needed to guide adult humans in rearing their young. It will include or imply some of that information, but actually, there is very little scientifically respectable evidence available that speaks *directly* to the topic at this point in history. What this book will do is to present and discuss most of what I know about the empirical data, and in addition call for a radical reorientation of our research efforts. It is my judgment that in spite of the presence of many very talented and well-meaning people in the field, research in child development is generally proceeding in a terribly unproductive and scientifically improper fashion.

It seems to me that we are wasting enormous quantities of talent and money.

Because I am convinced that the knowledge we seek is more important than that of most any other scientific enterprise and that the overall effort of the field leaves a great deal to be desired, I am writing this book with a sense of urgency.

I would like to express my deepest appreciation for assistance of several kinds over the last twelve years. Professionally, I owe a good deal to many people; in particular, I would like to thank Drs. Peter Wolff, J. McV. Hunt, and Harold Haynes, along with Mrs. K. Riley Clark, Peter Castle, and Richard Light. The staff at Tewksbury Hospital, especially Miss Helen Efstathiou and Mrs. Frances Craig, have been most helpful. Mrs. Mary Comita has performed secretarial chores valiantly. The Foundation's Fund for Research in Psychiatry gave me the support necessary to begin my research career. Finally, I wish to thank my wife and children who have been a constant source of strength and happiness.

The material in Chapters 4 and 5 produced by my colleagues and me has been supported over the past ten years by the following funding agencies: Grant M-3657 from the National Institute of Mental Health; Grant 61-234 from the Foundation's Fund for Research in Psychiatry; Grants HD-00761 and HD-02054 from the National Institutes of Health, the Optometric Extension Program; Grant NSG-496 from the National Aeronautics and Space Administration; Grant AF-AFOSR 354-63 from the Office of Scientific Research, United States Air Force; the Rockefeller Foundation; and was performed in part pursuant to a contract (OE 5-10-239) with the United States Office of Education under the provisions of the Cooperative Research Program, as a project of the Harvard University Center for Research and Development on Educational Differences.

Acknowledgment is made to the following for permission to reprint the indicated figures. FOR FIGURES 1, 8, 20, 21, 22, 23, 24, 25, and 26: From White, B. L., and Held, R. Plasticity of sensorimotor development in the human infant. In Rosenblith, J. F., and Allinsmith, W. (Eds.), *The causes of behavior: Readings in child development and educational psychology* (2nd ed.), pp. 61, 62, 65, 66, 67, 68, and 69. © Copyright 1966 by Allyn and Bacon, Inc., Boston. Reprinted by permission of the publisher. FOR FIGURES 2, 3, 9, 11, 12, and 13: From White, B. L., Castle, P., and Held, R. Observations on the development of visually directed reaching. *Child Development,* 1964, *35,* 349-64. Reprinted by permission of the Society for Research in Child Development. FOR FIGURES 4, 6, 28, 29, and 30: From White, B. L. Child development research: An edifice without a foundation. *Merrill-Palmer Quarterly,* 1969, *15,* No. 1, 50-79. FOR FIGURE 7: From White, B. L., and Clark, K. R. An apparatus for eliciting and recording the eyeblink. *Percept. Mot. Skills,* 1968, *27,* 959-64. Reprinted with permission of authors and publisher. For FIGURE 14: From Haynes, H., White, B. L., and Held, R. M. Visual accommodation in human infants. *Science,* 23 April 1965, *148,* 528-30, Fig. 1. Copyright 1965 by the American Association for the Advancement of Science.

1

INTRODUCTION

THE BOOM IN INFANT RESEARCH

IN THE LAST DECADE the field of developmental psychology has been experiencing an exciting renaissance. Certainly, one of the most vigorous sectors of this field is the study of the human infant. At the 1967 biannual meetings of the Society for Research in Child Development, approximately 20 per cent of all papers presented dealt with the behavior of normal human subjects less than two years old. There is an enthusiasm within the rapidly growing ranks of researchers in infant development which I find exciting and contagious. The increasing numbers of people, projects, reports, and positions available in this area certainly indicate that we are undergoing an extraordinary expansion.

Without doubt the most influential figure in the recent history of the field has been Jean Piaget. In my opinion, his truly remarkable work, especially the classic *The Origins of Intelligence in Children* (1952), has been the greatest single stimulus for the field. There have, of course, been many other important factors. It is probably not mere coincidence that the National Institute of Child Health and Human Development is the fastest growing National Institute of Health, and that heavily funded programs in early education such as Project Headstart and Parent-Child Centers have recently emerged. It is clear that the Zeitgeist is favorable to the study of early human development.

SCOPE OF THIS BOOK

In this day and age, no book of this sort can even pretend to be comprehensive. I, therefore, feel obliged at this point to go beyond whatever meaning attaches to the title of this book in defining its scope. This study deals primarily with the infant from birth to six months, the age span for which the large majority of work has been done. It concentrates on my work and that of my colleagues. It is frankly not comprehensive in terms of the entire span of infancy nor of all subject matters dealt with in the literature. In addition, it does not deal extensively with foreign work.

The substantive work on infant behavior (aside from that produced by my colleagues and myself), is presented in two sections: the first (Chapters 2 and 4) having to do with the behavioral phenomena of infancy, and the second (Chapters 3 and 5) having to do with how the experiences of infants influence their behavioral development. The numbers of behavioral phenomena that have been studied are very great, and the scope of such work has usually been very narrow, e.g., visual orientation, sucking rates, activity level, the pupillary response, etc. In addition, such studies have most often been performed with small samples and very narrow age ranges. The number of studies of experiential factors in infant development has, on the other hand, been very small. I have therefore dealt with the studies of behavioral phenomena by citing a good deal of the most important work and then summarizing what these and other studies seem to have taught us about the ethology of the human infant. In the case of the studies of the role of experience, I have briefly described what experimenters have actually done.

My plan is to introduce the reader to early human infancy as an ethologist such as Lorenz introduces a more exotic species (1965). I hope to go beyond Lorenz in several ways. I deal, albeit briefly, with the work of many investigators and attempt to provide some perspective on their work. Then, in the hope of stimulating reform, I try to describe what I perceive to be an unhappy state of affairs which exists in the field today. I follow with a presentation of what we know about the role of early experience in development, and finally, I introduce and discuss what I consider to be some of the interesting new issues in the field.

THE SIGNIFICANCE OF RESEARCH
ON HUMAN INFANCY

The major goal of developmental psychology is to generate the knowledge that will enable man to structure early experience so as to maximize the likelihood of optimal development for each child. Of course "optimal development" presupposes a value system, and value systems vary (Erikson 1950). Nonetheless, it is the primary responsibility of developmental psychologists to unravel the laws of the complicated process of human development, in order that a particular family in a particular society may know how to rear a particular child toward whatever developmental goals that family deems desirable. Such a purpose is, to me at least, as important as any other scientific goal imaginable.

Research on human infancy is, of course, a subarea within developmental psychology. Infancy, or the first two years of life, is of especial importance for several reasons. Logically, any inquiry into human developmental has to begin at conception. For practical purposes, birth is the earliest point at which intensive study may begin. Further, by virtue of the cumulative or epigenetic nature of human development, it has become clear that there can be no full understanding of human behavior at any point in life without knowledge of the history of the person. Finally, many lines of evidence suggest that infancy is probably a "critical developmental period" for many major processes including motivation, intelligence, language, and social and emotional development.

THE CASE FOR THE SPECIAL IMPORTANCE OF EXPERIENCE DURING INFANCY

Interest in this topic is a fairly recent phenomenon. Throughout recorded history, societal concern for structuring the experiences of young children has been manifested almost exclusively for children six years of age and older. A handful of pioneers such as J. Comenius, F. Froebel, and H. Pestalozzi sponsored education for four- and five-year-olds during the seventeenth and eighteenth centuries (Cole 1959), but it was not until the time of Sigmund Freud (1905) that Western society was effectively urged to attend to the influence of experiences during infancy. Subsequently, the work of J. B. Watson, Irwin, Arnold Gesell and others has added to the interest in this earliest period of life.

Probably the most potent spur to the present-day concern with infancy has been the early work of Piaget (1952, 1954). Piaget's remarkable studies of the intellectual development of his own three children during infancy have inspired a substantial number of modern workers. Perhaps the most vigorous proponents of Piaget's work on infancy have been J. McV. Hunt (1961) and John Flavell (1963). Hunt, especially, has made explicit the possibility (indeed, he believes it to be a virtual certainty) that the experiences of the first two years of life are of very great impor-tance for all that follows, but not everyone in academic circles shares Hunt's position. Many respected professionals have serious doubts about this thesis based in part on the frequently found low predictive value of developmental standing in infancy (Furfey and Muehlenbein 1932; Ander-son 1939; Bayley 1940).[1] That is, infants who appear precocious during infancy are, if anything, likely to score slightly below average on intel-ligence tests as adults.

At the same time that Piaget's work has been sparking a rebirth of interest in early intellectual development, a second line of inquiry into the effects of early experience has been undergoing a somewhat smaller but steadily growing renaissance. The question of the relationship of early experience to man's social and emotional behavior, which received a good deal of attention in the 1930s and 1940s (probably as a result of the influence of Freud) is now being reexamined. The science of ethology, the study of various animal species in their natural habitats, is being em-ployed along with Piagetian and Freudian ideas in a reconsideration of how humans develop their capacities to feel for and relate to each other (Bowlby 1958).

There seems to be an increasing sense that a study of moment-to-moment experiences during the first two years of life has much to teach us about these developments. This belief seems to be one consequence of a large number of studies of the mother-child relation (e.g., Ainsworth 1967; Moss 1967; Caldwell 1969; David 1961) including studies of ma-ternal deprivation (Spitz 1945; Bowlby 1951) and studies of early ex-perience in other species (Harlow 1962; Levine 1957; Denenberg 1967).

We have far too little evidence, collected with far too primitive measur-ing devices, to feel sanguine about any firm position on the importance of infant experience. Just as clearly, however, it is much too risky to assume that such experience is unimportant while waiting, perhaps for several decades, for sufficient evidence on the issue to accumulate.

If it should turn out that experience during infancy is of vital impor-tance, it would probably have the following kinds of consequences. Highly respected students of development such as Freud, Adler, Sullivan, Erikson, Bowlby, and Scott have all suggested that the social and emotional potential of any human may undergo serious irreversible damage during infancy. The emerging picture, though not based on a high compilation of direct evidence, suggests that the growth of the specific mother-child relation-ship begins sometime around the third month of life (Ambrose 1961).

---

[1] For an exception to this view see Knobloch and Pasamanick, 1960.

This most fundamental human bond is said to undergo crucial development during the following months. Along with the specific mother-child relationship (and apparently directly dependent upon it) is the more general capacity to relate to others and to experience and express affect. The voluminous literature on maternal deprivation and related topics seems to indicate clearly that gross inadequacies in early interpersonal experience can cripple (socially and emotionally) a child for life. While, mercifully, relatively few children undergo such extreme deprivation, this line of research indicates that interpersonal experience during infancy is of especial importance in the formation of the basic structures which subsequently mediate social experience throughout life.

As for other areas of development, Hunt (1961, 1965) has argued persuasively that intellectual capacity and intrinsic motivation are especially vulnerable during infancy. Hunt is not alone in this position; Hebb (1949) and Robert White (1959) have both spoken eloquently on this topic. In the area of language development, which is broadly acknowledged to be of fundamental importance for educational success, most research has concentrated on post-infancy periods. On the other hand, though elaborate productive language is rare during infancy, it has long been known (McCarthy 1954) that infants are capable of receptive language function during the second year of life. Few would doubt that the dramatic acquisitions in language during the third year of life depend significantly on language experiences in infancy. This question is unfortunately all but unexplored.

The current federal government sponsorship of Parent-Child Centers for infants is testimony to the growing belief in the importance of infancy for such developmental processes. Again, spokesmen often address their remarks toward the prevention of serious harm to children. The more subtle but probably more common moderate deficiencies that large numbers of presumably "normal" children suffer are also worthy of our attention. It is quite conceivable that our current standards of "normalcy" for young children will some day come to be viewed as unacceptably low. It will be surprising if several decades from now we have not learned how to structure the experiences of infancy so as to assure a far more interesting, pleasurable, and productive beginning for each child.

Man's study of his own kind has a history as old as civilization. Its most common expressions have been in literature and philosophy. Psychology, the scientific study of man, is comparatively new. Many psychologists date the onset of the field as 1879 when Wundt's laboratory was established in Germany. Infancy is a period of human development which has only recently attracted psychologists. Even today, considering how much there is to know, very little is actually known about the age range of six days to two and a half years.[2] This incredible fact is explained by another rather simple fact. Children in that age range are not readily accessible in groups. In the United States, once the newborn leaves his peers in the maternity ward at the age of five or so days, he doesn't roost with contemporaries again until he is at least two and a half years old, at which time he may (but probably won't) attend a nursery school or day-care center. Since, therefore, infants are primarily available only in their homes and only one at a time, studying them is expensive and inconvenient. This is probably the major reason that we are shamefully ignorant about infants. Clearly, however, if only out of sheer epistemic curiosity, the human race will not forever abide this curious gap in its knowledge of its own kind.

SPECIAL PROBLEMS AND ISSUES

The need for data

In this country, the most widely utilized source of information on the behavior of the human infant is probably the work of Arnold Gesell (1941). His schedules of development are at once widely used yardsticks for normal development and also outlines of development. Other infant behavior scales, such as those of Cattell (1940), Buhler and Hetzer (1935), and Bayley (1965), characteristically offer about the same degree of detail. The Griffiths scale (1954) is a considerably sounder instrument in terms of statistical test construction requirements, but isn't founded on a significantly better body of normative data. These instruments are designed primarily for diagnostic screening purposes. They usually cover most major areas of behavior including intellectual or adaptive behavior, motor, social, and linguistic functions. Typically, an infant's status in all of these very large domains is assessed in less than one hour. The infant is tested on 20 to 30 items, including information the mother is asked to supply on habitual performances in language, etc. Considering the complexity of each of these areas, it is patently obvious that infant tests such as these do no more than make a scratch on the surface of an extremely complex series of interwoven processes. A look at the analyses of modern linguistics such as that of Brown and Bellugi (1964), or of cognitive theories such as those of Piaget (1952, 1954), indicates the enormous difference between in-depth studies of infant capacity and typical screening practices. Further-

---

[2] In a recent editorial in a leading journal (*Child Development*), Alberta Siegel (1967) pointed out that during 1965 and 1966, of the 152 papers published in that journal only 15 reported data on subjects more than five days but less than a year old. Not a single paper published during that period concentrated on children of one to three years of age.

more, the in-depth assessments of infant capacity have barely begun. An enormous amount of hard work waits to be done in charting the development of the many sensory capacities, motor abilities, interests, etc., of infants. Traditional topics such as individual and sex differences or rates and ranges of development have as yet been dealt with only in the most preliminary fashion.

Study problems

It is only natural that the first focus of research in the growing field of infant development be on the various behaviors that infants exhibit. As described above, there is a need for vast amounts of information on the rapidly changing abilities and interests of the human infant, but knowledge of how infants behave will not suffice. We cannot afford to assume that experience is only of minor importance for the course of development. As parents, psychologists, educators, child welfare professionals, it is our responsibility to structure the environment of each child so as to maximize the likelihood of optimal development. In another publication (White, Castle, and Held 1964), it has been suggested that so-called "normative" data on development can only be assumed to be normative for subjects reared under the same general conditions as the standardization sample. In a report on the ontogenesis of visually-directed reaching, institutionally-reared infants exhibited mature reaching at about five months of age. In a series of subsequent experiments (White 1967), groups of infants were reared in especially designed environments, and they learned to reach by three months of age. For a species where the course of development is largely determined by genetic factors, the study of rearing conditions is, perhaps, of minor importance. For man, it is likely to be of profound importance.

To study rearing conditions means to study patterns of care-taking behavior, the physical surround, the social surround, the daily schedule, etc. Further, it means that these factors must be studied, as they change during the subject's development. The infant of less than six months is crib-based and cannot locomote. The infant of 18 months lives in a radically different world. The older infant usually changes his locus of activity many times each day. The six month old is considerably more a captive of a comparatively invariant set of physical conditions. Clearly, the study of the environment will be a much more complicated task than the study of child behavioral phenomena *per se*. This is not the end of the problem, however, for different environments may produce common experiences in children, whereas common environments may result in different experiences. As Thomas et al. (1963) point out, experience is a function of both external conditions and the nature of the experiencing organism. We cannot rely on a specification of a static set of rearing conditions if we seek understanding of patterns of early experience and their effects.

An enormous amount of work must be done analyzing the course of experience throughout infancy. Existing examples of this kind of study are the baby biographies of the past (Preyer, Shinn, cited in Wright 1960), the recent work of Church (1966), and especially the work of Piaget. Such work is so time consuming and so laborious that few undertake it, and one is inclined to despair. It is my contention (and I believe it undeniable) that to the extent that experience influences development, we *must* embark on many such studies.[3]

Even though we do not yet possess detailed knowledge about the fabric of infant experience, the topic of the effects of such experience has received attention from researchers for several decades. Indeed the hardiest perennial in the garden of psychological issues seems to be the nature-nurture or heredity-environment dispute. The topic is centuries old and has never been set aside for very long by either society or students of development. During this century we have seen the pendulum swing from an emphasis on what is inherited (Darwinism, instinct theory) over to the mechanisms of learning (e.g., I. Pavlov, R. Thorndike, J. B. Watson, etc.) then back to the role of maturation (e.g., A. Gesell) then back to the plasticity of early development (e.g., J. McV. Hunt, Project Headstart, etc.). Currently, the issue seems characteristically alive and controversial, with rebutters to the environmentalists in the areas of education (e.g., A. R. Jensen 1969) and ethology (e.g., E. K. Hess), and advocates in studies of learning (e.g., J. L. Gewirtz, L. P. Lipsitt), comparative studies (e.g., V. H. Denenberg), perceptual motor development (e.g., B. White), and social development (e.g., M. Ainsworth).

---

[3] Recently, two techniques for the quantitative analysis of on-going experience have appeared (Caldwell 1968; White 1969c).

2

THE CURRENT STATE OF KNOWLEDGE CONCERNING THE BEHAVIOR OF HUMAN INFANTS

INFORMATION ABOUT INFANT BEHAVIOR can be divided into two major categories: information generated from studies of human infants (direct evidence) and information generated from studies of adult humans and other species (indirect evidence). The most valuable data are indubitably from studies of human infants. It has become traditional to supplement such direct evidence with findings from studies of other animal species. For example, few would deny the usefulness of studies of vision in other mammals to the understanding of human sensory function; nor would anybody argue about the value of the information on the developing central nervous system that has come from studies of creatures as far removed from man as the horseshoe crab (Hartline 1949) or the frog (Lettvin 1959). On the other hand, certain cautions are necessary. Clearly, some topics such as the acquisition of language are explorable for all intents and purposes only through human subjects. In addition, though mammals share many characteristics, to generalize across species is always a risk. The carryover to human infants of such indirect evidence should therefore be treated as tentative until the time that *direct* confirmation can be obtained. The same caveat is necessary when evaluating evidence gathered in studies of humans older than infants. The classic example is, of course, the Freudian theory of infantile sexuality which has had enormous influence but was constructed out of studies of adults. The greater portion of that theory has never been confirmed by direct studies of representative populations of infants. This distinction between direct and indirect evidence is quite important for the consumer of knowledge about infant development. Except for Piaget's theory of the ontogenesis of intelligence (1952) and Gesell's concept of "reciprocal interweaving" (1941), none of the existent theories of infant development are rooted in studies of human infants. A case in point is learning theory as espoused by followers of Pavlov, Skinner, and Spence, etc. Classical, operant, or instrumental conditioning are commonly claimed to constitute the primary modes of learning in infancy, but this conception is based mainly on studies of adult humans, dogs, cats, rats, and pigeons (Lockard 1968). Very few learning theorists have made serious investments in an unprejudiced view of learning phenomena in infancy as a prelude to their work.

DIRECT EVIDENCE ON INFANT BEHAVIOR

Longitudinal studies

⌐Screening studies. These are characterized by brief overall examinations of large numbers of infants. Examples of such work are the studies of Bayley (1965), Buhler (1935), Gesell (1941, 1943, 1949), and Griffiths (1954). In each case, these researchers have produced monthly age norms from tests that can be administered to infants in less than an hour. A child's performance on any of these tests can be used to determine his general developmental progress. Characteristically, such test results cannot be used to predict performance in grade school or on standard I.Q. tests.[1]

⌐ Intensive studies of specific developmental processes. These are characterized by small numbers of subjects and biweekly observations and examinations of the same children over several months of life. To my knowledge, only three studies of human infants fit this description: Piaget's work on sensorimotor intelligence (1952), Thomas et al. on temperament (1963), and our own work on visual motor development (White, Castle, and Held 1964; White 1967).

⌐ Large sample, broad scope studies. Examples include the Berkeley Growth study and the Fels study. All such major American longitudinal studies have been succinctly described by Kagan (1964). These studies are the least intensive in dealing with individual infants and rearing conditions. Many of these studies gathered no data on infancy other than retrospective material. Those that did attempt to study infancy directly usually sampled the situation briefly once or twice a year. The procedure in the Fels study, for example, involved the administration of the Gesell

---

[1] But see Knobloch and Pasamanick, 1960, for a contrary view.

test and brief observations of mother-child interactions at six month intervals. Clearly, such studies have their primary value in directions other than a thorough understanding of the innumerable interactions of experience and development during infancy.

Cross-sectional studies

Perception. These are characterized by high precision, small sample size, and restricted scope. Most commonly, an individual researcher has studied isolated perceptual phenomena such as visual orientation, attention (e.g., Fantz 1962, 1964; White 1967; Lewis 1967; Koopman and Ames 1967), convergence (Wicklegren 1966); depth perception (Fantz 1961; Bower 1964; Polak 1964), form discrimination (Ling 1942; Hershenson 1964, 1965; Salapatek 1965), and shape constancy (Bower 1966) as these phenomena are influenced by various stimulus characteristics such as density of contour or brightness. Vision is by far the most frequently studied sensory modality. Very little has been done in audition (Eisenberg 1966), and almost no work has been executed in touch, taste, and other perceptual realms. Furthermore, the first 18 months of life have not received equal attention. The vast majority of work has been done on the child of less than one month of age (Siegel 1967), although within the last year or two the situation has been improving. A few researchers have attempted to trace the development of certain visual perceptual phenomena over several months during infancy (Fantz 1967; White 1967), but these are the exceptions rather than the rule. In summary, a major proportion of our research effort is currently devoted to molecular studies of visual perceptual function during very early infancy.

Learning. These are characterized by high precision, small sample size, and restricted scope. Many investigators in this field seem to believe that the only important kind of learning that infants are capable of is some form of conditioning. A major purpose of their efforts over the last several decades has been to demonstrate that infants can be conditioned at birth or soon after (Marquis 1941; Lipsitt 1963, 1966, 1967; Papousek 1961; Kaye 1965; Siqueland 1964; Lintz 1967; Fitzgerald 1967). Indeed, there have been attempts to condition infants in the womb (Spelt 1938).

Russian investigators have been at this effort longer than anyone else, probably because of the pervasive influence of Pavlov on their studies of human function. In general, they have had little success with newborns (Brackbill 1962). It is not until the third month of life that they have been able to establish discriminative responses, i.e., positive responses to one previously neutral stimulus and, in the same test situation, negative responses to a related neutral stimulus. The ability to establish such responses is potentially of great importance for the study of sensory capacities, a line of inquiry sorely needed by the field.

As it is, we now know (Gollin 1967; Horowitz 1968; Lipsitt 1967) that with enormous care and effort, under rigidly controlled laboratory conditions, short-lived conditioned responses can be established in newborns. This achievement is an important accomplishment from a technical point of view, but it is doubtful that it has taught us much about the conditions of learning in infancy. Few would doubt that infants learn an incredible number of things in the first two years of life, and it is quite unlikely that the kinds of circumstances demanded by the conditioning paradigm occur often enough in the life of any child to account for more than a small amount of what is mastered. It appears that research in this tradition has two other potential values for the field. As mentioned earlier, it may develop a powerful tool for the study of sensory capacity in the pre-verbal child; and, second, it may prove useful in therapeutic situations where short-term changes in behavior are necessary. As for the problem of understanding how infants learn, I believe we will have to look elsewhere.

Language. In spite of the fact that infants commonly acquire extensive receptive language skills during the second year of life and that the next year marks the sudden appearance of a variety of well-developed expressive language abilities, there has been insufficient direct study of the development during infancy (McCarthy 1954). The acquisition of primary aspects of language such as the earliest spoken and understood vocabulary has been thoroughly documented, although not on a wide variety of subcultural groups. More sophisticated studies of language such as those of Brown and Bellugi (1964) and M. M. Lewis (1951, 1963) either have not dealt with the first 18 months of life, or have concentrated on describing in detail the course of development of vocalizations. Although expressive language ability is ordinarily negligible during infancy, a good deal of work needs to be done in the area of receptive ability. An example of such work is Friedlander's studies of infants' preferences and discriminative abilities (1965). By giving an eight-month-old infant the opportunity to control his auditory feedback, Friedlander has, for example, been able to study the infant's ability to detect his mother's disguised voice. Receptive grammatical ability is another major topic that is as yet not thoroughly documented though some work is in process, e.g., A. Lillywhite at the University of Oregon and E. A. Ringwall at the State University of New York at Buffalo.

Personality. Again there have been comparatively few direct studies of personality development in infancy. The longitudinal studies of Thomas, et al. have been cited. P. H. Wolff has studied a small number of newborns for manifestations of affect and volition (1959). Sibylle Escalona has had a long standing interest in infant personality and was associated with the Menninger longitudinal study (1952, 1953). She and G. M. Heider have attempted (without much success) to predict adult characteristics from descriptions of infant personality (1959). Several years earlier Irwin (1930, 1932) and Fries and Woolf (1953) had studied differences in activity levels of infants, also with an eye toward prediction of later behavior. Campbell (1967) has recently reported on the same topic. Birns (1965, 1966), Crowell (1965), and Korner (1966) have worked on the problem of responsivity of newborns. Aside from these few efforts, one might guess from the literature that all infants were equally gay or dour, outgoing or retiring, stubborn or easy.

Social development. Studies of social development in infancy have concentrated on four topics: the smile, the mother-child interaction, fear of strangers, and attachment behavior. In fact, the first three are subsumable under the fourth, which has recently been receiving increasing attention. There have been numerous studies on the first three topics. Spitz (1946), Ahrens (1953), Ambrose (1961), and Polak et al. (1964) have examined some of the stimuli that elicit the ubiquitous smile of the 14 week old and the onset of this primary social phenomenon. Ainsworth (1967), Moss (1967), and a host of others have studied the mother-child relationship, long a favorite area of inquiry. Spitz and others have documented the "stranger anxiety" responses of the seven to ten month old (1945). Finally a provocative article by Bowlby (1958) and the general effect of the growing field of ethology have helped stimulate renewed interest in attachment behavior such as is illustrated in the work of Schaeffer and Emerson (1964).

A variety of relatively isolated but interesting studies of infancy should be noted. Prechtl has provided a good deal of information on instinct-like behavior patterns such as the rooting reflex in neonates (1958, 1965). Twitchell, a student of Denny-Brown, has studied the grasp responses in infancy for many years (1965a). Frances Graham and Rachel Clifton, following a classic line of investigation, have done extensive work on orienting and attending reflexes in newborns (1966). In fact, there have been many high quality molecular-scoped studies of infant (usually neonatal) function, such as the work of Pratt (1954) and Peiper (1961). Although space does not permit extensive citing of work in this field, the next section will be an attempt to summarize where we stand today on the subject of what infants are like, on the basis of direct evidence on the problem.

Summary and assessment

What then do we know about infant behavior on the basis of direct evidence? We know a great many things and yet only a small fraction of what needs to be known. Some important generalizations can now be stated with confidence. Infancy, for example, is a period of very rapid change. Not only is the behavior of the newborn quite unlike that of the eighteen month-old child, it is also clearly unlike that of the twelve, six, three and two month old; nor is this phenomenon restricted to the newborn. The behavior of the two month old is strikingly different from each of the others, etc. It is not until the second half of the first year that a month's time doesn't bring major behavioral changes.

Perception. The most extensively studied modality is vision. Especially during the last decade no topic has been of more interest to students of infancy than vision. The current view, stimulated by the work of Fantz (1961), is that the newborn human is capable of far more differentiated visual function than previously believed. The newborn when awake and alert (Wolff 1959) will at times definitely gaze at stationary visible targets if they are constructed of thickly drawn, highly contrasting contours (Fantz 1962; Salapatek and Kessen 1965). He will also exhibit a rudimentary capacity for visual motor pursuit (Dayton and Jones 1964; Wolff and White 1965). By six weeks, flexible visual focusing begins and ability is fully developed by four months (Haynes, White, and Held 1965). Bower reports evidence of depth perception and size constancy at two months (1964, 1966). Fantz's data (1962) indicates an increase in acuity from about 20/400 at birth to 20/70 by six months. The development of visual alertness during the first five months has been plotted by White (1967).

Audition, the second most popular sense modality, has received very little attention over the years (Eisenberg 1966). Recently, Eisenberg (1969), Bartoshuk (1962), and Friedlander, McCarthy, and Soforenko (1965) have reported respectively on auditory function in the neonate and in the eight month old. The general picture is that, as in the case of vision, the newborn is able to function in rudimentary fashion, although he is far less capable of making discriminations than adults are able to make or than he will be able to make at six months.

The other sense modalities of taste, smell, touch, the vestibular sense, and kinesthesis have received little attention recently, although Engen and Lipsitt (1965) using conditioning techniques reported that neonates can discriminate primary olfactory sensations. Additional information about perceptual function is available from older studies cited in Pratt (1954) and Peiper (1963). Such information is mostly in the form of highly technical reports on neonatal function which do not markedly alter the picture of the neonate as a naive, primitively organized processor of sensory information. In contrast, by the end of the sixth month, the infant seems to have achieved functional use of most primary perceptual systems.

Learning. One could easily write several hundred pages on this topic, especially if the term is defined to include more than just the results of conditioning studies. If there is any one thing that characterizes human infancy, it is learning. That the infant can be conditioned even as early as the first week of life no longer seems disputable. The work of Lipsitt and his colleagues seems to establish that point thoroughly. Gradually, during the succeeding months, the range of responses and ease of conditioning increase as shown by the work of many, especially Papousek (1961), Brackbill (1967), Rheingold et al. (1959), Gewirtz (in press), Lipsitt (1963), and Weisberg (1963).

The development of intelligence, defined crudely as problem-solving capacity, and its related elements such as object permanence, causality, means-ends behavior, perception of time, has been studied most extensively by Piaget (1952, 1954).

Piaget's work has had enormous influences on modern research, and during the next decades we shall unquestionably see hundreds of studies extending his efforts. In Piaget's view, the newborn is essentially nonintellectual, totally incapable of intelligent or purposeful (means-end) behavior, but he is designed to take in and be modified by experiences. At six months or so, the infant shows primitive intelligence in the form of means-end behavior but still does very little of what we call "thinking" or manipulating of ideas. By eighteen months, true ideation or mental representation begins to supplement and replace immediate action as the primary mode of coping with problems. Support for this view has been provided by some recent studies of sorting behavior (Ricciuti 1964; Ricciuti and Johnson 1965). Infants twelve to twenty-four months of age, when given the opportunity, reveal classificatory behavior in the sequences with which they handle small objects, indicating that some sort of mental organization is guiding their play. A similarly important metamorphosis is characteristic of other cognitive developments such as the conception of causality, time, etc., during this comparatively brief period of infancy.

Language. Although expressive language in infancy has received a fair amount of attention, there isn't much of it to talk about (McCarthy 1954). Newborns cry and gurgle; four month olds babble and play with sound utilizing their own saliva. The first meaningful word (for the types of children who have been studied) has commonly been found at any time from as early as seven or eight to as late as forty months of age, with twelve to eighteen months most frequent. If the eighteen month old has two-word sentences, he is considered to be doing well. The growth of linguistic meaning has been studied by Lewis (1951, 1963).

Receptive language, on the other hand, has been much less investigated. That the child can hear well enough to discriminate words and inflections by the time he is six months old is highly probable, though not well documented (Friedlander 1965). In fact, in a recent survey Eisenberg (1966) has described auditory research in infancy as "a vast wasteland." If we grant the likelihood that the infant is listening to and processing language with increasing facility from six months on and juxtapose the fact that shortly after eighteen months he routinely reveals a surprisingly rapid acquisition of complicated expressive language skills, it strongly suggests an important learning from six to eighteen months. It is a serious indictment of researchers in infancy that this is another largely unexplored domain.

Personality. Here again the picture we can portray contains little more than broad outlines. For various reasons there has never been a great deal of interest in the direct study of infant personality. All the leading theories of personality deal with infancy by a process of generalization from older subjects and speculation. Beginning with Freud and moving on through Adler, Jung, and Sullivan and then on to Erickson, no major theorist has had extensive direct evidence on the topic of personality in infancy. Part of the problem lies in the difficulties of conceptualizing personality traits and problems for this age range. Additionally, there is the previously mentioned difficulty of obtaining subjects.

Though direct approaches have been very rare, the topic has been indirectly approached in various ways. Studies of maternal deprivation (Bowlby 1951; Casler 1961; Yarrow 1961, 1964) indicate that rupturing the infant's maternal bond leads to expressions of loneliness and apathy in late infancy. Work on social development (see next section) hints at the special attractiveness of the infant's first smiles to adult humans (Spitz and Wolf 1946; Ambrose 1961, 1963), and also of the likelihood of apprehensiveness coincident with the "stranger anxiety" reactions at about eight months (Morgan and Ricciuti 1968).

Perhaps the most direct attack on the problem of personality development of infants is the work of Thomas et al. (1964). In a long-term, intensive longitudinal study, some 130 infants are being followed from birth to well beyond infancy. Personality characteristics such as activity level, mood, and persistence are being assessed at monthly intervals. From this study, information on individual differences, continuity of temperament, and differential stimulus effects on parents of these children will be forthcoming. Aside from this one study, however, I know of no others of this type except for the older longitudinal studies. As for the latter, because the investment in data collection for individual children has been extremely small for the period of infancy, they have not provided detailed information on early personality development.

Social development. For the first four to eight weeks of life, the infant is essentially presocial. It is not until the second month of life that the first smiles in response to the human face or voice can be easily elicited. Fortunately, most new mothers don't really notice this potentially depressing state of affairs. By the time the mother is emerging from the typical pleasant emotional haze of giving birth and getting used to having an exciting new dimension to her life, the child has begun to smile regularly; nor is she aware that there is apparently nothing personal in these early smiles. For many weeks infants smile indiscriminately. It is not until the fourth month that there are modest preferences exhibited for the mother's face and voice (Ambrose 1961). It is an interesting fact that of several hundred primarily institutionally-reared four-month-old infants I have observed, all but two or three would smile readily in response to the gradual appearance of any human face at a distance of about twelve inches (except of course when they were sleeping or very distressed). This is but one symptom of the general positive mood that characterizes infants of this age. It makes them very pleasant to have around and very desirable as subjects for behavioral research. At seven to nine months, the classical stranger reaction usually (but not always) appears (Ricciuti 1968; Morgan and Ricciuti 1968). Bowlby (1958) has suggested that this phenomenon signals the end of the "catholic" phase of social function and the beginning of a solidification of primary family ties. Little is known about social behavior in the second year of life, but my guess is that a great deal of social learning is taking place during that time. Piaget has suggested that, through innumerable explorations of objects and their attributes, the infant is learning the "me, not me" distinction. This cognitive achievement along with the emergence of conceptions of permanent objects with existences of their own must be extremely important for social development (Decarie 1965). In addition to such related factors, infants of this age appear to be very much interested in people, their gross actions, and the nuances of their different facial and vocal expressions. The primary object of this interest is ordinarily the mother probably because she spends more time with him by far than anyone else.

Curiosity. An example of a topic of fundamental importance for human development is the development of curiosity. Curiosity is an "intrinsic interest in learning," and, of course, an understanding of how this human attribute develops would be most desirable. Very little direct study of the process has been undertaken.

Infants normally first exhibit what may be labeled curiosity at about two months of age. Along about this time, the infant becomes considerably more interested in his surroundings than in the first month of life (Gesell 1941; White 1967). In his interest in the nearby scene, in human faces, and, most strikingly, in his own hands, he first shows what looks like curiosity. At about eight months, the infant exhibits a particular interest in tiny particles (Schwarting 1954).

Again, when it comes to the details of the development of curiosity, especially after the first half year of life, with the exception of some new work on the five to nineteen month old by Charlesworth (1963, 1966), there is virtually no evidence. Recent observations strongly suggest that there is no more interested creature alive than the eighteen-month-old infant (White 1969c). Perhaps if psychologists knew more about this period, we might be able to help more children maintain this apparently normal infant enthusiasm for learning that is diminished in so many children by the time they reach school age. I doubt if a more important educational problem exists.

General behavioral development. In *Developmental Diagnosis* (1941), Gesell provides a series of valuable brief characterizations of infants as they develop during infancy.[2] These descriptions are based largely on the performance of 107 infants on the Gesell screening test, and though they are informative, they are limited by the nature of the Gesell test. This test, called the Gesell Developmental Schedules, consists of 20 to 30 items designed to cover all major phases of behavior; partly because of its broad purposes, it does so in a rather superficial fashion. For example, there is no comparing the sophistication of the Hunt-Uzgiris' scales for assessing cognitive development (Uzgiris and Hunt 1966) with the four to six items utilized by Gesell for the purpose. Nevertheless, the Gesell descriptions are about the best we have in the way of longitudinal ethological data of infancy.

INDIRECT EVIDENCE

Related studies of adult humans

Motivation and personality. For most of its brief existence the field of infancy has been significantly influenced by the work of Freud, his followers (e.g., Ferenczi, Abraham), and opponents (e.g., Adler, Jung), and their descendants (e.g., Sullivan, Erikson). In 1905 Freud published his theory of infantile sexuality. This paper described the psychosexual stages of the first years of life. Infancy, for example, was described as the "oral" period, the mouth being the prime locus of activity through which

---

[2] Another source of such information is the work of C. Buhler and H. Hetzer (1930).

the sexual instinct found satisfaction. Ferenczi (1924) and Abraham (1921) elaborated on these conceptions, and up until the emergence of the influence of Piaget in this decade, no ideas were as influential as Freud's in shaping research and practice in infancy. A fundamental flaw in this situation was that the ideas were not rooted in studies of infants. The course of early development of specie-survival factors such as the urge to procreate is still largely unknown. Its newer form seems to be the study of attachment behavior (e.g., Bowlby, Ainsworth, Emerson, and Schaeffer). Few people now believe that either recollections of neurotic adults or exclusively theoretical approaches are likely to shed much light on infant development. The concept of phylogenetic continuity, on the other hand, has survived and led to empirical comparisons of infancy in various species (Scott 1968; Newton and Levine 1968).

Perception. In a series of ingenious experiments, Held (1961) has attempted to generate a theory of perceptual-motor development in man based largely on studies of adult human function. Recently he has studied development in kittens (1963) and monkeys, but the primary basis for his theory has been his earlier work. Held has induced adults to relearn perceptual-motor skills by systematically altering the feedback consequences of limb and body movements. He has found that it is easier to lose and reacquire eye-hand accuracy than eye-body coordination. He has therefore concluded that the latter is more fundamental, with eye-hand coordinations mapped on to eye-body space in original acquisition. Unfortunately for the theory, however, though human infants cannot locomote until the second half of the first year, they can visually guide their hands to nearby objects quite accurately as early as two months of age (White, Castle, and Held 1964). I have taken the trouble to describe this disagreement, not because Held's theory has yet been very influential in the field but rather to demonstrate the limited generalizibility of theory which isn't derived from direct studies of the phenomenon in question.

Another case in point concerns current adultomorphic assumptions about the exclusively social meaning of the first smiles. Piaget noted that his infants often smiled at toys and their own hands as well as at faces (1952). In our work we, too, have often observed smiling at such objects. These and other observations restrict speculation and suggest more promising interpretations, such as Piaget's notion that the first smiles are at least in part a sign of recognition of familiar visible patterns.

Related studies of other species

A synonym for the title of this section is "comparative studies." Some treatment of these topics is necessary because (1) such studies have influenced and will continue to influence the field of human infancy, and (2) few would deny the principle of phylogenetic continuity. Of course, the field is far too large to be discussed in detail in this book; I will therefore treat only what I perceive to be the most important points of contact with work on humans.

Social development, imprinting and maternal relations. There are several good summaries available on the extensive research on these topics (Newton and Levine 1968; Eibl-Eibesfeldt 1967; Moltz 1960; Gray 1958; Hinde 1966; Ambrose 1963). Imprinting, or the early exclusive social attachment to another creature (usually the mother), has been a popular topic for study for several decades. In general, most researchers seem to agree that the human infant goes through some process similar to the imprinting seen in birds and dogs. This process, which may be completed in a matter of hours in geese, apparently takes many months in man. The first easily visible manifestations are in the indiscriminant smiling of the three month old (Ambrose 1961). The other major indications are the stranger reactions of the last half of the first year (Morgan and Ricciuti 1968) and the tendency to cling to the mother especially in strange circumstances during the first half of the second year. It seems likely that Bowlby (1958) and others are correct when they claim that this process is of fundamental importance for future social function and emotional health. Since much of the attachment process presumably takes place between six and eighteen months, however, we have very little direct evidence on the topic as yet. A solid beginning effort has been made by Ainsworth (1967) and Schaeffer and Emerson (1964) in particular.

Motivation, instincts, drives, and curiosity. The provocative work of the ethologists, Lorenz (1965), Tinbergen (1968), Hinde (1952), Mason (1962), on other species, especially on instinctive behavior, is a constant reminder that man probably does not come into postnatal existence in a totally unformed psychological state. So far the search for complicated invariant motor sequences in human infancy parallel to nest-building and web-weaving in other species, has been brief and unsuccessful (Tinbergen (1968). I frankly doubt if we will ever find in humans more than vestigial remains of elaborate instinctual motor patterns, such as the simple rooting, smile, and grasp responses of early months of life. Few would deny, however, the probable relevance of ethological ideas in the prime survival areas of man's existence such as procreation and self-defense. In retrospect, Freud's early attempt to use comparative ideas to explain infant behavior in terms of the sexual instinct seem less appropriate than Bowlby's (1958) attempt to integrate notions from ethology, psychoanalysis, and Piaget.

In general then, we are left with the notion that the exploratory tendencies of the human infant, noted by Piaget (1952), Gesell (1941), Fantz

(1964), and B. White (1967), are indeed consistent with results of studies of numerous other species (R. White 1959). About the so-called "primary" drives, there has never been any doubt that much of infant behavior is motivated by hunger, thirst, avoidance of pain, etc.

Over the last several decades, much has been learned about the structure and function of the sensory system from studies of other species (Granit 1947; Kuffler 1957). Recently, pioneering work by Hubel and Wiesel (1962) and Lettvin (1959) has provided interesting suggestions, for example, about the way vision may operate in man, as a result of their studies of retinal activity in the eye of the cat and the frog. In general, while such researchers do not claim that human function is identical to that of other species, few would deny the value of such work for increased understanding of human function.

Summary and assessment

The fact of phylogenetic continuity must be reckoned with in any study of human development. At the beginning of this century, in a wave of enthusiasm for Darwinian ideas perhaps, the influence of comparative ideas was very strong. In the work of MacDougall, for example, the concept of instinct was used to "explain" a great deal of human behavior. Freud and Lorenz, in particular, have had a very large influence on studies of human development. This early enthusiasm waned, however, and in ideas such as those of John B. Watson and J. J. B. Morgan (1917) the pendulum seemed to have swung the other way during the twenties and thirties. Since then, with the help of increasing amounts of direct evidence on infant behavior, we seem to be undergoing a rapprochement, with the influence of comparative studies assuming a more moderate level. The modern view seems to be that man is an unfinished creature at birth, with many fragments of instinct-like behavior and basic drives which are biologically guaranteed but are subsequently molded and differentiated by experience.

3

THE CURRENT STATE
OF KNOWLEDGE
CONCERNING
THE ROLE OF
EARLY EXPERIENCE

INFORMATION ON THE EFFECTS OF early experience on infant development is variegated and sparse. In the early stages of a science, attention is necessarily focused on outcome phenomena (or dependent variables, to use the technical term). There have been more studies, for example, of the abilities of infants than there have been of their experiences or rearing conditions. Partly due to the logic of inquiry which stipulates that one must identify the diverse manifestations of the topic of interest and then investigate causal factors, and partly due to the historical de-emphasis of the importance of learning, surprisingly few studies of early human experience have actually been executed.

DIRECT EVIDENCE

Natural experimental (correlational) studies

There are three major types of studies of this kind. Although they are not commonly labeled natural experiments, this label seems to be appropriate and useful. The inevitable diversity that exists in the developmental histories of children makes it possible to do post hoc statistical analyses which can serve as valuable preludes to the use of true experimental methods.

Screening studies. The greatest investment of talent and funds has been in longitudinal studies of the large sample, long-term variety cited earlier. Generalizations about the value for good human development of accepting, democratic mothers, for example, are the kind of information generated by such studies. An intensive analysis of these studies is reported in a recent provocative book by Bloom (1965) which claims that early experience, especially during infancy, is of vital importance for development. In a widely quoted passage, Bloom states that 50 per cent of intelligence, as commonly measured at age 17, is achieved by age four (p. 68). This simple statement has captured the imagination of many readers. By and large the thesis of this chapter is sympathetic to this general position, but it must be noted that any implication that we are currently able to measure human intelligence with precision is unfortunate. To talk about 50 per cent of something presupposes its accurate identification, which has not yet been done for the "intelligence" of infants and young children. Further, it assumes that the half of "intelligence" mastered by the four year old is equal to the half acquired throughout the rest of life. This assumption is clearly misleading.

In the same book (Bloom 1965, p. 78) an attempt is cited to characterize the major environmental factors in early development. Thirteen "process variables" are listed which presumably cover the topic of environmental influences on the development of intelligence. One such "variable" is the "availability of books"; another is the "emphasis on the use of language in a variety of situations," etc. Such analytical efforts require a great expenditure of energy in digesting the voluminous results of the longitudinal studies. They are not without merit, but they should not be taken as indications that we are generally knowledgeable about early experience and developmental processes. The fact is that the longitudinal studies on which the analysis rests heavily were not designed to provide detailed information on the processes of development. The Fels study, for example, made the following investment in infancy:

1. Gesell tests at 6, 12, 18, and 24 months.
2. Interviews with the mother, annually from birth.
3. Two- to four-hour observations of mother-child interactions every six months from birth.

This data base is about average for the infancy period for the longitudinal studies. Contrast this investment of less than 30 hours per infant for the first two years of life for *all* behavioral development with the several thousand hours of effort by Piaget in trying to understand intellectual development during infancy. Clearly, the longitudinal studies provide only the barest outlines of knowledge about environmental influences on infant development.

Deprivation studies. The second class of natural experimental data is the deprivation study. A large number of such studies evaluating the effects of the absence of the mother during the early years have been summarized by Bowlby (1951), Casler (1961), and Yarrow (1961, 1964). Although the scientific quality of the studies is highly variable and often open to serious criticism, the weight of the evidence overwhelmingly suggests that the absence of the mother for more than three months during infancy (beginning after the first six months) has serious negative consequences for the infant's social and emotional development. The question of the irreversibility of the effects, is largely unexplored at this time.

What it is about the mother's absence that is important is a matter of some debate. Spitz, who wrote the pioneering article on the topic (1945), claimed that the cause of the problem was the serious disturbance of the developing mother-child libidinal bond. This position stemmed directly from Freudian notions about the development of the sexual instinct in infancy. If the two major motivational forces in infancy are the sexual and aggressive instincts, and if the mother is seen as a central link in the chain of discharge of sexual energy, then clearly her removal is catastrophic. Yarrow and Casler, on the other hand, impressed by the literature from studies of other species emphasize that maternal deprivation also usually means a drastic reduction in opportunities for learning and exposure to varied stimulation. Their view is more consistent with that of Hunt (1961) who points out that even if the mother is present throughout infancy, a child may be severely deprived if the opportunity to confront appropriate variations in circumstances is not provided. Somewhat in contradiction to the aforementioned point of view, are the findings of an early study by Dennis and Dennis (1941). In an experiment which probably could not be performed today, the Dennises reared a pair of fraternal twins from the end of the first to the end of the fourteenth month of life under conditions of "restricted practice and minimum social stimulation." With very few exceptions, the behavioral development of these infants was largely unaffected by what appeared to be a significant degree of long-term deprivation. The Dennises also reported (1940) that severe restrictions on motor practice in early infancy produced by the cradling practices of the Hopi did not seem to retard the onset of walking. Dennis and Sayegh's (1965) and Dennis and Najarian's (1957) more recent work with larger samples in an institution for infants in the Middle East has tended to provide more support, however, for the environmentalist's position.

In my view, the mother could be absent in the first three or four months of life with no harmful aftereffects, if suitably designed nonsocial experiences were made available to the infant. Of course, the mother's presence is potentially a much more human and efficient way of meeting the child's needs (as any father of a breast-fed child will testify).

Cross-cultural studies. The third type of natural-experimental study of environmental effects is the cross-cultural study. The work of Erikson (1950) is one example of such research. In such work various national characteristics have been attributed to patterns of child rearing. At this point in history, very little in the way of useful detailed knowledge about experience in infancy has come from such studies. They do hold much promise for future work.

Experimental work on the effects of early experience

Studies of this kind fall into two distinct categories: those that manipulate infant experience over periods of less than an hour and those that cover longer periods of time. Short-term studies are far more common for several reasons: (1) they are less expensive to execute, (2) rigorous experimental control over human experience is feasible only for such brief periods, and (3) society is quite ambivalent about scientific "tampering" with human experience, especially that of helpless and possibly vulnerable infants. Unfortunately, though they are far more numerous than long-term experiments, it is highly questionable whether one can generalize extensively the findings from brief, laboratory-like teaching sessions to the issue of the complex cumulative effects of experience in real life.

Short-term studies. Examples of short-term manipulations of experience are the studies of Rheingold et al. (1959) and Lipsitt et al. (1967). The former have performed one study to determine whether responsiveness by an adult to the vocalizations of three-month-old infants could affect the frequency and distribution of those vocalizations. Infants were given operant conditioning training for 27 minutes for each of two days, and it was clearly shown that vocal output could be made contingent upon social reinforcement (smiling, touching, and vocalization by the experimenter). In a follow-up study (1959), Rheingold and Bayley tested 14 of the original sample of 16 children some 12 months after their experimental experience to determine whether there were any lasting social effects. In brief, they found no evidence of carryover effects. They also pointed out, however, that in spite of their early institutional experience (X duration = 9.2 months) the infants appeared to be developing normally. Lipsitt et al. (1966, 1967) have performed a series of conditioning studies which have indicated that the sucking and head-turning behavior of neonates and various behaviors of older infants can be conditioned to previously neutral stimuli. Their studies feature very careful control over test circumstances to ensure that no extraneous stimulus is likely to interfere with the effect of the conditioned stimulus, e.g., a pure tone. With great technical skill they have demonstrated that this form of learning is within the infant's capacity. Unless reinforced trials continue, however, the effects are very short-lived. However, nothing very close to the experimental conditions is likely to occur with regularity in the ordinary life of an infant. Therefore, it is more likely that such studies will find their primary value in problem areas such as diagnosis and short-term behavioral control than in the analysis of long-term experience and development. As cited earlier, extensive reviews of this type of study are available.

Long-term studies. Studies of this sort are still in short supply. Ourth and Brown gave neonates 300 extra minutes of handling during the first four days of life (1961). They were hoping to lessen the shock of transition from the womb, where the child regularly experienced movement through space and various vibrations from the mother's body, to the crib where the infant is mostly immobile. They found virtually no effect of extra handling on crying patterns (the primary post-experimental behavior examined). Salk (1960), too, performed a study aimed at easing the neonate's transition from inter-uterine to post-natal existence. He exposed 102 newborn infants to a taped, loud (85 DB) heartbeat sound (72 beats/minute) for 24 hours a day during weeks 1-4 and 9-12. He reports that experimental babies gained significantly more weight during the first four days of life and cried considerably less than control infants ($n = 112$) during periods when the heartbeat sound was provided.

Rheingold (1956) provided individual mothering (from 9-4, 5 days/week) for a group of eight, six-month-old institutionally reared infants for an eight-week period. She found evidence of social attachment for the experimental mother but no evidence of increased "stranger anxiety" in the experimental group. Neither did she find significant improvement in postural, "adaptive," or "intellectual" behavior in post-test performance.

That some form of learning *can* occur during the first week of life has been demonstrated by the teaching experiments of Lipsitt, et al. (1967). That some of learning *does* occur was demonstrated by Marquis (1941). Eighteen neonates were put on a four-hour feeding schedule. Sixteen other infants were put on a three-hour schedule. At day nine, the three-hour group was changed to a four-hour schedule. Measures of motor activity showed that the three-hour group had adapted to the three-hour schedule.

Casler (1965) provided small extra amounts of tactile stimulation to a group of eight institutional infants (stroking the middle part of the body) for 20 minutes each day from week 22 to week 32 and found modest general developmental acceleration (according to Gesell test scores) to be a consequence. Casler performed a parallel study with the same design where the experimental treatment was a sober, continuous repetition of number recitation to the infant's midsection (i.e., one, two, three, four, five, one, two, etc.). Ten weeks of such "enrichment" produced no detectable effects.

Fantz (1967) suspended one of two small colored objects over each of the cribs of 10 home reared and 10 institutionally reared infants from 3 to 24 weeks of age. The familiar object was paired with a novel target and a 20 second test of the infant's preference was made each week from 3 to 10 weeks and twice monthly from 16 to 24 weeks. No significant experiential effects were found.

My colleagues and I have performed a series of related enrichment studies over a period of eight years (White 1967, 1969b). This research, which included four experimental and two control groups (average number of subjects, 15) featured the special arrangement of physical circumstances and activities in which the infant lived, 24 hours a day, from birth to four and a half months of age. (These studies are reported in detail in Chapter 5.) Enrichment procedures included extra handling, practices designed to increase head-rearing, swiping at appropriate objects, visual exploration and prehension, the provision of interesting and developmentally appropriate forms and objects in the infant's immediate surround, and the provision of red and white striped mitts designed to make the infant's hands more perceivable.[1] The consequences of these various procedures have repeatedly supported the idea that experience can play an important role in early development. Primary sensorimotor developments such as visual exploration, hand regard, and visually-directed reaching, appeared to be very sensitive to such changes in rearing conditions. Even rudimentary cognitive foundations seem quite open to influence from such apparently innocuous environmental factors (White 1969a).

Greenberg et al. (1968), following up on this work, reports acceleration of the blink response to changes in visible stimulation as a consequence of continuous exposure to objects somewhat similar to those utilized in the work of White (1967) et al. Ten home reared babies were provided with stabiles over their cribs from their sixth to their fourteenth week of life. The visually-based blink response subsequently came in at about eight weeks as opposed to eleven weeks for controls.

Earlier it was noted that Dennis and Dennis had reported that minimal social nurturance and opportunities for practicing emerging skills seemed

---

[1] The various experimental conditions or enrichment procedures in this series of studies were designed primarily on the basis of several years of observational work with similar infants, the results of each of the experiments, and a general intent to provide environmental conditions that would mesh with the emerging interests and rapidly changing abilities of such infants.

to be generally adequate to support normal infant development. Dennis and Najarian have subsequently reported two studies on infants reared in an institution in Lebanon. In the first of these studies (1957), various infants were tested throughout the two to twelve months age range with the Cattell scale. In addition a group of four and a half to six year old children who had been reared in apparently similar ways in the same institution were tested with the Goodenough draw-a-man, Knox cube, and Porteus maze tests. Serious retardation was found increasingly throughout the first year, but the older group was only slightly inferior to a comparison home reared group. While not denying the likelihood of deficits in language-related areas in the older children, the writers point out that the fairly serious retardation of the first year apparently did not lead to parallel serious deficits four years later.

In a second study, Sayegh and Dennis (1965) tested the hypothesis that the deficits seen in the institutional population during the first year of life were attributable to inadequate learning opportunities. Five, seven to twelve month old infants, were given one hour of supplementary practice for fifteen days to accustom them to the upright position, to encourage interest in objects, and to develop manual skills. Their rate of development (measured by scores on the Cattell test) was four times that of controls although they were still severely retarded. Furthermore, when supplementary training ceased, so too did the developmental enhancement.

Field experiments

Both the short- and long-term experimental studies cited in the preceding sections can be characterized as intervention research. What they featured, despite varying styles, was control over some segment of the infant's history of experience. In each case control involved a careful designation of the experimental treatment and the rationale for its design. In addition control meant that the experimenter monitored the study himself either by applying the experimental treatment or by closely supervising the situation. In each case the number of subjects was quite small except where the experimental treatment was very simple as in the Salk study (i.e., the provision of a recorded heartbeat). Another kind of intervention study should also be discussed. Here I refer to two older studies and a handful of newer projects sponsored by the recent antipoverty social action programs.[2] Though it might be argued that this group of studies is not clearly different generically from the last, I would like to see the distinction made for reasons which should become clear in the discussion

---

[2] The studies by Irwin, Skeels, Schaeffer, and Caldwell, were performed with subjects more than six months of age.

that follows. The most extensive and advanced projects of this type are the recent studies of Gordon at Florida State University (1969) and Schaeffer in Washington (1969). Other studies of this kind are the infant projects of Weikart at Ypsilanti (1969) and Caldwell at Syracuse (1969). The older studies are those of Irwin (1960) on the effects of reading stories to infants, and of Skeels (1956) on the rearing of institutional infants by retarded women.

Irwin (1960) had working-class mothers read stories to their infants (in their own homes) for 20 minutes a day from the time the infants were thirteen until they were 30 months of age. These children showed significant increases in produced speech sounds.

Skeels reported in 1956 on the later development of a group of 13 subjects who as young infants had undergone institutional rearing and, beginning at about 18 months of age (range 7.1 to 35.9 months), had spent an average of 18.9 months in an "enriched" atmosphere. The enrichment consisted of living as "house guests" in a home for retarded women rather than in the conventional orphanage. Most of the experimental group was placed into adoptive homes shortly after the experiment ended. Follow-up studies were conducted 2½ and 21 years later. Though the age at first admission and length of stay at the orphanage in early infancy was quite variable, all experimental subjects appeared retarded ($\bar{X}$ I.Q $= 64.3$) prior to the enrichment experience. At the end of the enrichment period, their development had accelerated dramatically ($\bar{X}$ I.Q. $= 91.8$) in contrast to controls ($\bar{X}$ I.Q. $= 60.5$). Two and a half years later their improvement had increased ($\bar{X}$ I.Q. $= 95.9$), and 21 years later the group was grossly normal, in sharp contrast to the control subjects. In Skeels's opinion, within the general enrichment situation, the intense one-to-one relationship which most of the experimental infants formed with the retarded women was the core factor underlying the positive results.

The newer projects attempt to preclude poor early development by providing a broad heterogeneous pattern of enrichment experiences to home reared, low-income infants. As such they are at once directly relevant to the concerns of society and simultaneously less controllable and interpretable than the more conventional experimental work. If they produce excellent results and if they record, in detail, how they did it, society can reproduce their efforts. On the other hand, since it is impossible to exercise a great deal of control over the many experiential factors involved, it is most difficult to determine the varying degrees of effectiveness of the numerous intended or unintended enrichment factors. (The Skeels study is, in many respects, similarly constituted, and Skeels points out that his pin-pointing of the personal relationship factor can only be considered as a strong hunch.)

Schaeffer trained 8 college educated women to tutor low-income negro infants in their homes. For a 21 month period, beginning at 14 months of age, each of these tutors averaged just under 4, 1-hour a day private sessions a week with each of 20 infants. They concentrated on verbal stimulation using books, toys, and anything available to maintain the infant's interest. The experimental treatment was frankly opportunistic and evolutionary. The effects on development were striking. Average I.Q. gains (at 36 months) over controls were 17 points. Equally significant results were obtained on measures of linguistic and perceptual development. In spite of the expense, the results seemed well worth the effort.

Gordon's project has been even more ambitious. He has aimed at more than affecting infant development. His goal was to produce a recipe for intervention that would be economically feasible. He, therefore, trained low-income women with modest educational backgrounds to tutor mothers of infants who ordinarily would develop very poorly. Gordon's program featured a series of "learning games" for mothers to play with their infants beginning in the first months of life and continuing throughout infancy. These games were designed on the basis of whatever ideas seemed reasonable in the light of general modern psychological thinking. For example, Piaget's sensorimotor theory (1952, 1954) and its application in the work of Uzgiris and Hunt (1966) and Escalona and Corman (1968) was the basis for many of the games. General ideas about the virtue of extensive exposures to words as labels and as cues to physical differences among objects were the basis for other games. Finally, certain items from standard infant tests were utilized. These ideas plus any others (e.g., the pat-a-cake game) were used to provide the means whereby mothers would become more sensitive to infant development and would be encouraged to devote considerable time to training and, presumably, enjoying their infants. Preliminary results are modest but encouraging, especially for female subjects. Scores on the Griffiths' infant scale indicate about a 6 point overall gain for girls and a nonsignificant 1½ point gain for boys. Subscores in the areas of hearing and speech and eye-hand activity were the most substantial.

Gordon seems to trade impact on infant development for parent involvement and feasibility. As for experimental control, one cannot expect such an action-oriented program to resemble for example, the laboratory based studies of vocalization rates.

Two other studies should be cited. Caldwell at Syracuse has recently operated a small experimental day-care center for low-income families. Home reared infants received a general pattern of supportive, personal treatment from the time they were 6 months old for at least 24 months during work hours. An attempt to measure the effect on the development of mother-child attachment behavior indicated no differences as compared with a home reared non-day-care group. This finding was interpreted as supportive of the general feasibility of the day-care remedial experience in that the bond between mother and infant was not weakened by such experience.

In Ypsilanti, Michigan, Weikart has been engaged in intervention research with three- to six-year-old low-income children for some seven years. Recent findings have stimulated him to begin work in infant enrichment. Although no written reports are yet available, I have cited his work because of the extraordinarily high quality of his work with older children. I would recommend that those interested in infant care practices for such children request information directly from Weikart.

The opportunity to perform long-term controlled interventions is quite rare. Further, such studies, of necessity, cannot be nearly as rigorously controlled as short-term studies. They are, however, obviously directly focused on the questions those responsible for rearing infants want answered. I believe much more work of this kind should and can be done.

Summary and assessment

The volume of direct, detailed knowledge of the role of experience in the development of the human infant is very small. What American behavioral science has so far invested in the problem represents a bare scratching of the surface of a few facets of a very complicated and extremely important scientific and social problem. I respect the studies of brief experiences of infants as legitimate and valuable scientific inquiries, but I do not believe that they can substitute for a direct attack on the larger issues. I believe a new methodology is needed to deal even in a preliminary way with the study of early experience, and I have tried to describe such an approach (White 1969b). I do not believe that extensions of the short-term approach which feature chaining of discrete stimuli with single responses will ever lead us to an unravelling of the interrelationships among the many stimuli simultaneously impinging on an infant at each moment, the cumulative effects of the multitudinous sequences of such moment-to-moment experiences, minute after minute, hour after hour, etc., and the numerous developmental processes *simultaneously* being affected by such stimuli.

INDIRECT EVIDENCE

Related studies of adult humans

In an indirect manner, the work of Freud and Sullivan and their descendents has influenced our views of the role of experience in early development. Concepts such as "birth trauma" (O. Rank) and the resultant hypersensitivity of some psychiatrists, pediatricians, and parents to the *special* short-lived but all-determining early experience seem to have had a widespread influence. The presumed importance of the mother's behavior vis-à-vis the establishment of healthy psychosexual behavior has likewise had enormous popular effect. Aside from such generalizations, however, the psychoanalytically inspired literature has taught us little about specific relationships between early experiences and developments.

In the area of perceptual development, however, several researchers have proposed explanations of specific experience-development relationships. As yet, these extrapolations from studies of other species have produced conflicting views of perceptual development. Held (1961) argues vigorously for the importance of early motor experiences within figured sensory surrounds, claiming that neither an interesting world nor self-induced movement, by themselves, are sufficient for optimal development. Riesen (1958) also recommends (though for different reasons) motor behavior in the presence of a variety of visible stimuli. Fantz (1964), on the other hand, has been impressed along with Bower (1964) by how much human infants are capable of perceiving about their visual worlds prior to extensive experience.

At present, there is no overriding, consistent message on large issues of perceptual or perceptual-motor development in human infants from studies of other species. It is, however, a very popular research area, and we can expect important results from this field in future years.

Related studies of other species

Numerous students of animal development have contributed to our thinking about the role of early experience in human development. They can be divided into two groups, those who believe that genetic factors are very important, and those who assign such factors relatively minor causal significance. Of the former group, the ethologists such as Lorenz and Tinbergen and the comparative psychologists such as J. P. Scott are good examples. Among the latter group are the descendents of Pavlov, Thorndike, J. B. Watson, Hull, and Spence such as Gewirtz, Lipsitt, and Siqueland (Associationists) and various other researchers such as S. Levine, Harlow, Held, and Hein.

The ethologist's position. Lorenz has argued most forcefully for increased concentration on the genetic contributions to human behavior (1965). He, like Piaget, has shown much less interest in and, in fact, some contempt for the topic of early experience. Clearly, it would be foolish to ignore the virtual certainty that some portion of the human behavioral repertoire is genetically guaranteed. Still, the evidence for complicated invariant motor sequences is quite sparse (Tinbergen 1968). We are left, then, with a reminder that at the very least we are likely to find some portions of early development essentially nonmalleable by environment manipulation. Beyond this statement there is little to say until someone with an ethological orientation uncovers dependable evidence of instinctive behavior in infancy which goes beyond the well-known instinct fragments like rooting, grasping, and stereotyped smiling.

Aside from the declaration that much of behavior is genetically determined and relatively impervious to experience, this group of researchers does suggest that certain rearing conditions are at least instrumental in the "normal" development of innately programmed processes. The ethological concept of the "critical period" which has received a great deal of attention (Scott 1968; Newton and Levine 1968; Ambrose 1963) has important ramifications for child-rearing practices. I have already cited Bowlby's analysis of the development of "attachment" during infancy. A necessary conclusion from this ethologically rooted line of inquiry is that child-rearing practices, out of respect for the fundamental requirements for human, social, and sexual development must ensure that adequate attachment behavior is encouraged in the first two years of life. The many studies of mother-child relations during infancy are relevant here (Ainsworth 1967; Caldwell 1963; David 1961; Schaeffer and Emerson 1964).

The associationistic position. Research in this tradition has been extremely popular throughout this century, both here and abroad. Its primary message, as best exemplified in the work of Gewirtz (in press), is that the key to the understanding of how an infant develops lies in the analysis of the environmental reinforcements which are contingent upon the infant's behavior. Gewirtz has therefore carefully studied care-taking practices in different cultures trying to identify the patterns of reinforcement which account for the likelihood of certain infant behaviors' being increased while that of others is reduced. This concentrated focus on environmentally-based reinforcement is only interrupted in such research by the necessity to identify some of the behavior repertoire of the child and at least a few of his needs or interests in order to have the essential prerequisite information for conditioning studies. Very little attention is paid to the possibility of genetically determined specie characteristics, or to the interrelationship among experiences, or any idiosyncratically developing mental structures of the kind Piaget calls "schemas."

So far, serious attempts within this tradition to deal with more than an hour of highly controlled experience have not been attempted for infancy except by Gewirtz. Repeated episodes of shaping behavior of older children and of psychotics have produced encouraging therapeutic results, but to show that behavior can be altered by concentrated training does not prove that infants ordinarily or primarily learn in the same fashion.

Other related studies. Certainly the literature on the effects of extra "handling" on laboratory reared mice, kittens, and monkeys has relevance for the subject of early experience in man. Levine, Denenberg, and others have repeatedly shown that small extra amounts of handling of infant mice have surprisingly general and significant beneficial effects (Reisen 1958; Denenberg 1967). The implication here is that previous views that the human infant should be touched as little as possible in early infancy for fear of traumatizing him may be in error. The few studies of the effects of handling human infants (Ourth and Brown, 1961; Casler, 1965; White and Castle 1964) seem to support the notion that benefits are more likely to accrue than serious damage from the natural impulse of mothers to cuddle their young infants. The results of the well-known work of Harlow on rhesus monkeys are also consistent with this conclusion (1962). Similar results have also been found with Siamese kittens (Meier 1961).

Finally, Held and Hein have performed an ingenious study to assess the role of self-induced movements in structured visible surrounds on perceptual-motor developments in kittens (1963). Although the study was only done on a small number of kittens and no replications have been attempted, the results suggest that efforts to facilitate motor activity within interesting environments would be developmentally beneficial for human infants.

Summary and assessment

Studies of adult humans have yielded relatively little detailed information to guide child-rearing practices. Scholars interested in social and personality development have provided provocative statements mostly in the form of caveats, such as the idea that the infant is establishing primary libidinal bonds and one should be quite careful to ensure that this process is not seriously disturbed, or that the infant is establishing a basic sense of trust or mistrust, etc. It is quite likely that there is a good deal of truth in statements such as these, but until now they have probably produced more anxiety than guidance in child rearers.

Studies of adult perceptual function have produced conflicting views on the role of experience in early development, although even those who feel that innate factors should be given greater emphasis would not recommend desisting from providing for sensorimotor experiences for infants.

Studies of other species have offered considerably more specific recommendations for infant experience. The work of the ethologists, though again devaluing the role of experience in general, does indicate that those who rear children should at least not inadvertently get in the way of the playing out of genetically preordained patterns of development. They warn of the danger of not providing adequate environmental conditions (at the proper time) to insure that common mammalian survival functions such as social attachment proceed adequately.

The associationistic tradition, stemming from the pioneer conditioning studies of Pavlov and Thorndike, seems to provide at least one primary idea of direct relevance to child-rearing practice. That idea is that consequences of an infant's behavior that occur with regularity are likely to exert an influence on the particular behavior in question. If, for example, a mother systematically ignored a baby's crying over several weeks, especially after the first few months, one could expect the child to be gradually less inclined to seek attention by crying. Likewise, if only the shrillest cries were attended to (over many such instances), one would expect the child gradually to develop a tendency to increase the loudness of his cries in subsequent states of need, etc. Again, I should like to emphasize the notion that redundancy, the repetition of many consistent experiences, seems necessary in order for important effects to result. The occasional or once in a lifetime experience is probably quite inconsequential most of the time.

The thrust of the other cited studies of nonhuman animals seems to be quite consistent with Hunt's thesis that the best way to rear an infant is to be knowledgeable about his rapidly changing abilities and interests and to arrange his environment and schedule so as to provide sequences of experiences that are suitably matched to those developing characteristics, starting immediately at birth.

4

RECENT ADDITIONS
TO WHAT WE KNOW
ABOUT
INFANT BEHAVIOR

SCOPE AND BACKGROUND OF THE
NEW DESCRIPTIVE DATA

WHY, YOU MIGHT ASK, can we not assume that everyone knows about the human infant and his living circumstances? After all, infants are everywhere. The incredible fact is that though human infants are all about us, they are almost unknown from an ethological or an ecological point of view. For example, until 1965, investigators had no notion of the visual focusing abilities of infants. One consequence was that the numerous visual preference studies triggered by Fantz's work (1961a, 1961b) were designed with no sense of how far one should place targets in order that infants of various ages might achieve clear images on the retinae, to say nothing of adequate perception.

As for the topic of what interests infants, I have seen several frightfully expensive research operations wherein the investigator had unquestionably promised a funding agency that he would condition infants to do X, Y, and Z, even though said investigator had little idea of infants' operant response repertoire and next to no knowledge of the kinds of rewards that infants work for. The results have been unworthy of a research field aspiring to scientific status. Such conditions seem to be rampant in the field of human development and must be corrected. Further, new researchers in this field should make an honest effort to become knowledgeable about infants before attempting experimental work with them.

Piaget's studies of the ontogenesis of intelligence in his own three children (1952) are unparalleled in this field. Characteristically, he invested thousands of hours with his subjects. If you ask an American developmental psychologist how much time he spent with each subject in his last study, you will find the average will be less than a half hour. If you ask for the sum total spent with infants in all studies he has ever done, the total might be less than a hundred hours. Furthermore, these few hours constitute his entire professional exposure to infant behavior. Finally, there will have been a minimal diversity of conditions during those times, because the infant had to be hastily put into the apparatus or test situation, hastily tested, and hastily returned to his own crib or his mother. Such is the normal background of researchers in human infancy.

We need much more work of the kind Piaget has done in advance of more sophisticated experimental work. We need the quality, intensity, and breadth of his work executed with substantial numbers of subjects and directed toward *all* major developmental processes, not just intelligence.

I was extraordinarily fortunate in being able to study physically normal infants living in relatively invariant environmental conditions at a local institution for illegitimate children.[1] The physical circumstances of the infant's world during the three-week to approximately four-month period are pictured in Figure 1.

Routine care consists of bottle feeding and diaper changing every four hours and a five minute bath each morning. Aside from such treatment, infants of that age and younger are left alone and usually supine.

My early studies were oriented toward (1) a solid sense of what infant behavior was like in that world and (2) identifying developments and experiences worthy of quantitative assessment. Fairly early in the game, I selected for study in addition to visually-directed reaching and its precursors, visual exploration, hand regard, visual pursuit, and visual convergence. Later the prerequisite function of visual accommodation and the diagnostically interesting blink response to approaching targets were added. A wide variety of other behaviors, such as postural developments, were to be handled by regular administration of the Gesell scales. As for experiences of consequence, many facts stood out rather readily. Among them were: (1) The first month of life is a poor time to study visual-motor function, at least under routine conditions. My subjects were only visually alert about 5 per cent of the time during the daylight hours. (2) Hand regard is a surprisingly popular activity. Most infants spend dozens of hours at it, especially during the third month of life (Fig. 2). (3) Tactual exploration with the hands is minimal until the third month of life, prob-

---

[1] I owe a large debt of gratitude to many people, especially Peter Wolff for that opportunity.

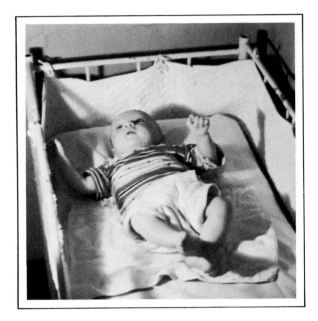

FIG. 1 The typical nursery ward facility for control infants.

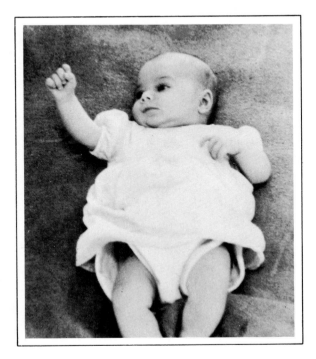

FIG. 2 Hand regard.

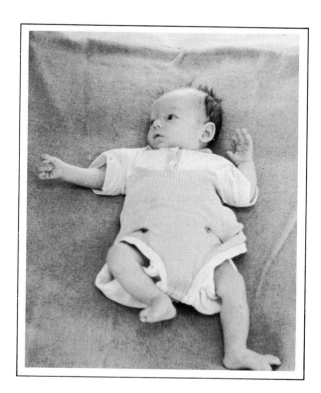

FIG. 3 The tonic neck reflex (TNR) posture.

ably because the modal position of the fingers up to that time is flexion and also because the tonic neck reflex virtually precludes mutual explorations by the hands (Fig. 3). (4) Most infants are visually alert and easily pleased during the third and fourth month of life. (5) Young infants are considerably less oral than psychoanalytic theory would lead one to believe.

THE PROBLEM OF QUANTITATIVE TECHNIQUES

I have never felt that our field is overpopulated with good tests or apparatus for assessment purposes. The best nonspecific instruments available seem to be the Griffiths scale and the Northwestern Infant Intelligence Scale by Gilliland. The latter had died aborning, and, Dr. Griffiths insisted that researchers take a six-week course in England before she would send them any materials. As a result, in spite of its weaknesses, I've used the Gesell schedules. I've also used the Rosenblith modification of the Graham scale to screen newborns. After testing 200 babies and never detecting one defective baby with the test that we couldn't spot with the naked eye, we dropped the test from our screening procedures.

For behaviors such as visual exploration and accommodation, there were no established techniques. We therefore devised our own. Although powerful because they are all custom-built for an infant's specific stage of development, they are of uneven overall quality because of heavy reliance on subjective measurement. My policy has always been to measure as well as I can what I believe merits measurement, rather than to measure only what I can measure with unquestionably high precision.

Visual attention, hand regard, and postural phenomena were assessed primarily through observation of typical activities in the ward. Such a technique has come to be known as "naturalistic observation." Some people are put off by the use of the ambiguous term "naturalistic," but by convention it has come to refer to observations where the researcher attempts to intrude as little as possible into the ordinary activities of his subject.

Naturalistic observation clearly has its limits. One cannot simply wait for the repeated occurrence of the behaviors of focal interest, nor can one afford to leave uncontrolled the circumstances under which they occur. Therefore, guided by what we were seeing in the wardroom, and also by various suggestions from the literature, we constructed a number of standardized test situations. These situations are designed to elicit samples of abilities at various points in their evolution. Aside from the three-hour watches which constitute the situation in which we assess the sheer amount of visual-motor behavior engaged in, we have tested for visually directed reaching (White, Castle, and Held 1964), visual accommodation (Haynes, White, and Held 1965), blinking to a rapidly approaching object (White and Clark 1968), and general development (using the Gesell schedules).

Each of these samples of behavior has been chosen because of its fundamental bearing on the infant's overall capacity to perform sensorimotor interactions with his environment. With the exception of the performances elicited by the Gesell test procedures, these behaviors constitute basic tools normally prerequisite to early explorations and information processing. They are complicated sensorimotor responses deliberately not dissected but treated globally in order to preserve their psychological meaning. Analytical studies such as the analysis of monocularly mediated responses are not being pursued at this time, because we believe that narrowing of the focus of this work would be strategically premature.

Visual exploration or attention. To assess the sheer amount of visual exploration, we used a subjective technique which consists of weekly three-hour, continuous watches of each subject. With the use of a rather simple definition of visual alertness—eyes more than half open, direction of gaze shifting within thirty seconds—and criteria for ruling out periods of moderate to high distress, we have been able to achieve inter-observer reliabilities in the nineties after very brief training periods (White and Castle 1964).

Prehension. For plotting the emergence of visually-directed reaching we instituted a standardized test session on a weekly basis. Details of the procedure are available in a recent paper (White, Castle, and Held 1964). In summary, this procedure also relies on subjective assessment of behavior, but unlike visual exploration we have not attempted to assess inter-observer reliabilities. We depended on consensus between tester and recorder which of course is not much better than conventional clinical testing. We did go beyond the Gesell procedure by designing a more attractive stimulus object (White, Castle, and Held 1964), and presenting it at 45° right and left as well as the midline and by using an extension rod rather than the hand with which to offer the object.

Visual accommodation. In a 1965 paper (Haynes, White, and Held), we reported preliminary data on the development of focusing ability in infants. Expertise in measurement in that first study was provided by Harold Haynes, a skillful research optometrist from Pacific University. The assessment technique utilized was an adaptation of a rather common procedure

TABLE 1   DYNAMIC RETINOSCOPY RELIABILITY DATA

Age (days)	Target Distance (inches)	N_s	Inter-observer Agreement Range (diopters) 0–½	½–1	1–1½
21–60	5	18	N_s 5	7	10
			% 27.8	31.9	55.6
	8	18	N_s 11	13	15
			% 61.2	72.3	83.4
	16	18	N_s 2	8	11
			% 11.1	44.4	61.4
			$\overline{X}$% 33.4	51.9	68.8
61–105	5	14	N_s 4	8	11
			% 28.6	57.2	78.7
	8	14	N_s 8	10	12
			% 57.0	71.6	85.8
	16	15	N_s 8	13	13
			% 53.3	86.9	86.9
			$\overline{X}$% 46.3	71.9	83.5

in testing the vision of adults. After my verification that the infant was attending to the target, Haynes would make a subjective judgment of accommodative performance with a retinoscope, and then check that judgment by using lenses of known power to standardize the appearance of the infant's response. (The procedure involved the testing of each eye separately.) Occasionally, I would check the results; but, at that time, my skill was so rudimentary that I could only verify readings under ideal conditions. Nonetheless, I was not reluctant to accept Haynes's statement that he had confidence in his results, especially since certain other behaviors were routinely consistent with his assessment of accommodative status.

We are now completing the analysis of a replication of the earlier normative study, an inter-observer reliability study, and an attempt to enhance the development of accommodative ability. In general, Haynes's normative

FIG. 4 The blink-eliciting apparatus set up on a conventional hospital crib with infant within test chamber.

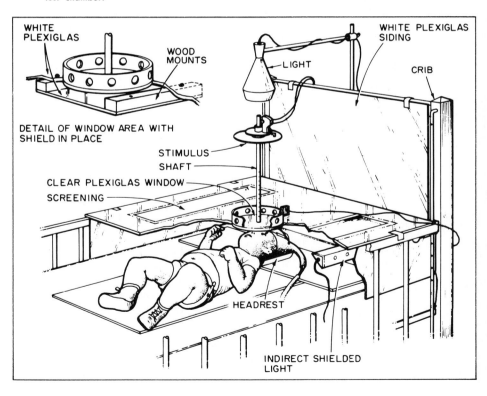

data appear to be confirmed, although inter-observer reliabilities vary as a function of age of subject and test distance (see Table 1). Unquestionably, dynamic retinoscopy is a difficult technique. My colleague, Dr. Zolot, an experienced optometrist, and I trained for about a year, testing three or four subjects a week, before we began formal data collection.

The palpebral response (the eyeblink) to an approaching visible target. We have managed to devise a reasonably sophisticated objective assessment procedure for this response (Figs. 4, 5, and 6). A polygraphic record of stimulus and response is obtained which is sensitive enough to allow fairly precise analysis of latency and amplitude as well as frequency of response (Fig. 7).

Our methods of measurement on the independent variable side of the ledger have been even less sophisticated. Most commonly, we have used duration of application of an experimental procedure. For example, in one study we administered 20 minutes of extra handling a day for 30

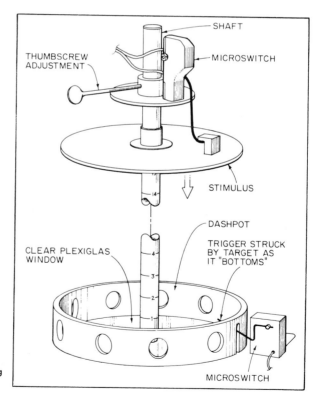

FIG. 5 Details of the blink-eliciting apparatus.

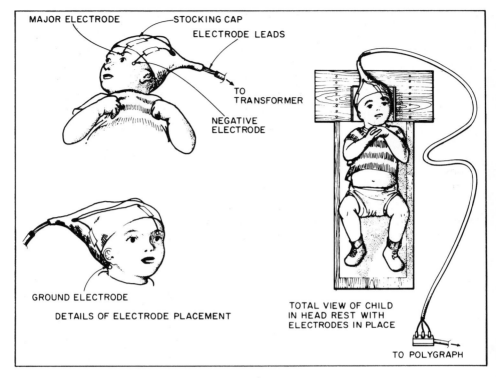

FIG. 6 Details of the electrode placement for the blink test.

days. In another, we have placed infants in prone posture in front of interesting visible displays for 15 minutes after feeding 3 times each day for 85 consecutive days. Another method we have used is simply to change the environment in a particular way at one point in an infant's development and let him live in that world 24 hours a day, until such time as a new sensory surround is called for. In such a case there is an added measurement that should be taken, because the extent to which subjects undergo different experiences as a consequence of an experimentally changed surround is quite variable. For example, in one study, two-thirds of the subjects viewed and batted the experimental objects repeatedly over a 30 day period, but the other third hardly even noticed them. Obviously, counts of such behaviors are a more accurate gauge of the functional value of the experimental conditions than the crude statement of duration of exposure.

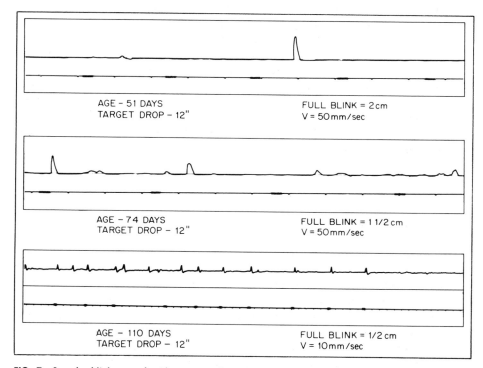

AGE – 51 DAYS
TARGET DROP – 12"

FULL BLINK = 2cm
V = 50mm/sec

AGE – 74 DAYS
TARGET DROP – 12"

FULL BLINK = 1 1/2 cm
V = 50mm/sec

AGE – 110 DAYS
TARGET DROP – 12"

FULL BLINK = 1/2 cm
V = 10mm/sec

FIG. 7 Sample blink records. The upper channel indicates eyelid activity while the lower channel is a record of stimulus action; the thicker sections indicate onset, duration, and cessation of a dropping target. The scale of the record for the 110-day-old infant has been compressed in order to illustrate the sterotopy of the behavior at that age.

SUBJECTS

Our subjects were infants born and reared in an institution because of inadequate family conditions. These infants were selected from a larger group after detailed evaluation of their medical histories [2] and those of their mothers, along with relevant data about other family members whenever possible. Only physically normal infants were used. Reports based on studies of institutionally reared infants generally include a statement acknowledging atypical conditions. In addition, such a group of infants

---

[2] Infants' daily records were screened for signs of abnormality under the supervision of Drs. Peter Wolff and Lois Crowell, who used standard medical criteria. Mothers' records were examined for possible genetic pathology and serious complications during pregnancy or delivery.

may constitute a congenitally nonrepresentative sample. On the other hand, two factors make a group of such infants unusually suitable for experimental research: First, rearing conditions are virtually identical for each infant, in marked contrast to the highly variable conditions for subjects reared in their own homes. Second, it is possible to systematically change rearing conditions in the institutional setting and to maintain continuous surveillance over them.

Figure 1 illustrates the typical nursery ward facility for infants between the ages of one and four months. Clearly the world of these infants is bland and uniform.

NORMATIVE DATA ON CONTROL INFANTS [3]

Visual attention

Procedure. A continuous three-hour record of visual attention and motor activity was kept, starting one hour after feeding. The observer was not seen by the infant throughout the period of observation. Visual attention was scored as the percentage of time an infant spent exploring his visible environment while awake, alert, and lying supine in his crib. An infant was judged visually attentive if his eyes were more than half open and their direction of gaze shifted within 30 seconds. Intervals during which these criteria were met but in which the infant was either unduly fussy or engaged in vigorous thumbsucking were not scored as time spent in visual exploration. Such intervals were most likely to occur during the last half hour of an observation period as the time for the next feeding approached. Forty-six per cent of the observations of visual attention were gathered by the author and the remainder by five different assistants. None of the assistants was aware of which infants were in the experimental group, although the author was. An analysis of the distribution of the scores about the median values revealed no significant differences among observers. (A subsequent inter-observer reliability test yielded a correlation co-efficient of $+.96$.)

Figure 8 illustrates the development of this activity from birth through four months of age; each point represents the average of two scores taken during successive two-week periods. It is interesting to note the corre-

---

[3] The data presented here were all gathered on infants reared at Tewksbury Hospital. Although in many respects, especially concerning the first three months of life, these data are consistent with what little detailed evidence we have on other populations, strictly speaking they are presented as "normative" only for infants reared under functionally comparable circumstances.

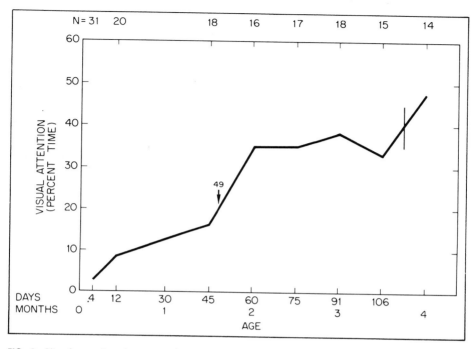

FIG. 8 Visual attention data—control group. The arrow at 49 days indicates the median age at which sustained hand regard appeared. The vertical bar at about 110 days indicates relocation to large open-sided cribs.

spondence between rather dramatic changes in the visible environment and the shape of this curve. For example, the sharp increase in slope between 45 and 60 days of age occurs at about the same time as the onset of sustained hand regard (49 days). For the next six weeks or so, the child spends much of his waking time observing his fist and finger movements. The next major change in the visible environment occurred for these infants between three and a half and four months (see vertical line on Fig. 8) when they were transferred to large, open-sided cribs. The combination of greater trunk motility, enabling them to turn from side to side, and the more diverse visual surroundings gave them access to a much more variable stimulus array. About this time, the slope of the curve again shows a sharp increase.

Perhaps the greatest return from this time-consuming procedure is a level of knowledge about individual subjects and group behavior at various ages that one rarely attains in conventional experimental work. Of central importance is the insight gained into idiosyncratic state patterns in subjects. Escalona (1962) and Wolff (1959) have both emphasized the importance of the state variable in infant work. I would not only endorse their views, but also suggest that until such time as we have highly refined objective measures of state, there is no substitute for getting to know infant subjects well. The second dividend from the practice of weekly watches is a generalized understanding of or feeling for different levels of functioning during the first half year of life. Any person who has worked with large numbers of infants during that age span knows that development proceeds rapidly. Newborns, for example, are strikingly different from six- or even four-month-old infants. Such a fact means that the practice of lumping data gathered on young infants who vary in age by more than a few weeks is a poor one.

One important revelation for me which resulted from these weekly observations was that, contrary to my academically bred expectations, infants weren't really very oral during the first months of life. In fact, between two and six months, a far more appropriate description would be that they are visual-prehensory creatures. We observed subject after subject spend dozens of hours watching first his fists, then his fingers, and then the interactions between hands and fingers. Thumb-sucking and mouthing were rarely observed except for brief periods when the infant was either noticeably upset or unusually hungry.

Visually directed reaching [4]

The prehensory abilities of man and other primates have long been regarded as one of the most significant evolutionary developments peculiar to this vertebrate group (Darwin 1871). In man, the development of prehension is linked phylogenetically with the assumption of erect posture (thus freeing the forelimbs from the service of locomotion), the highly refined development of binocular vision, and the possession of an opposable thumb, among other specializations. One important accompaniment of the development of prehension is man's unique capacity to make and utilize tools. Considering the acknowledged importance of these developments in phylogeny, it is surprising how little is presently known about the acquisition of prehension in man.

The detailed analysis of the development of a sensorimotor function such as prehension inevitably raises a classic theoretical problem. The human infant is born with a diversified reflex repertoire, and neuromuscular growth is rapid and complex. In addition, however, he begins immediately to interact with his postnatal environment. Thus we face the complex task

---

[4] I am indebted to my colleagues, Drs. Castle and Held, for much of the material in this section.

of distinguishing, to the extent that is possible, between those contributions made to this development by maturation or autogenous neurological growth and those which are critically dependent upon experience or some kind of informative contact with the environment. Previous work in the area of prehension, variously oriented in regard to this theoretical problem, has resulted in the gathering of selected kinds of data, namely, those kinds deemed relevant by each particular investigator to the support of his point of view on the development of prehension. Our own point of view is focused primarily around the role that certain kinds of experience have been shown to play in the growth and maintenance of sensorimotor coordinations (Fantz 1961). Consequently, we have focused our attention on gathering detailed longitudinal data of a kind that would aid us in eventually testing specific hypotheses about the contributions of such experience to the development of prehension.

Halverson (1932) studied the reaching performance of infants, beginning only after the onset of what we have come to consider a rather advanced stage in the development of prehension (sixteen weeks). Gesell (Gesell and Amatruda 1941) used the response to single presentations of a dangling ring and a rattle as items in his developmental testing procedures. These tests were designed to be used with subjects as young as four weeks of age, but prehension was of only peripheral concern to Gesell. These workers subscribed to the theoretical position, championed by Gesell, that most if not all of early growth, including the development of prehension, is almost exclusively a function of progressive neuromuscular maturation: an "unfolding" process. This view undoubtedly contributed to their neglect of the possible significance of the role of input from the sensory environment and to their stress on normative level of performance per se, rather than the relation between a level of performance and its behavioral antecedents.

Piaget (1952) made a number of original observations on the development of prehension, including the earliest stages of the process, which are prior to three months of age. His data are somewhat limited since his subject group consisted only of his own three children. And, as with Gesell, Piaget's interest in prehension was peripheral to another concern, namely, the sensorimotor origins of intelligence. Piaget's theoretical approach differs considerably from that of Gesell, being concerned primarily with the cognitive aspects of development. His work is focused on the adaptive growth of intelligence or the capacity of the child to structure internally the results of his own actions. As a result, he has formulated a theoretical point of view that centers around the interaction of the child with his environment, an approach similar to our own. This interaction is seen by Piaget as giving rise to mental structures (schemas) which in turn alter the way in which the child will subsequently both perceive and

respond to the environment. By conceptualizing development as an interaction process, this point of view avoids the oversimplified dichotomy of
maturation versus learning. Without the aliment provided by the environment schemas cannot develop, while without the existence of schemas the
environment cannot be structured and thus come to "exist" for the child.

Some primitive sensorimotor schemas are, of course, present at birth,
the grasp reflex and visual-motor pursuit being two that are particularly
relevant to prehension. Both Gesell and Piaget describe the observable
development of the subsequent coordination between vision and directed
arm and hand movements, part of which is clearly dependent on some kind
of practice or experience. Gesell, however, contented himself with a vague
acknowledgment of the probable role of experience in development, whereas
Piaget attempted to determine in a loose but experimental fashion the
role of specific kinds of experiences and structured his theorizing explicitly
around the details of the interaction process.

Piaget takes the position that informative contact with the environment plays an important role in the development of spatial coordination
and, in particular, prehension. The work of Held and his collaborators
(Held 1961; Held and Bossom 1961; Held and Hein 1958; Held and Hein
1963; Held and Schlank 1959) on the development and maintenance of
plastic sensorimotor systems in higher mammals, including human adults,
has led to a similar point of view. These laboratory studies have addressed
themselves to the question of which specific kinds of contact with the
environment are required for the maintenance and development of accurate
sensorimotor abilities such as hand-eye coordination. This work constitutes
a more rigorous experimental approach to some of the same kinds of problems that Piaget has dealt with on the basis of his extensive observations
and seems likely to be relevant to the ontogeny of prehension in particular.

It was with this general background in mind that we undertook the
study of prehension. In studies of animal development (Riesen 1958) the
technique of selective deprivation of environmental contact has been successfully used to factor out critical determinants. Since human infants
obviously cannot be deliberately deprived, other experimental strategies
must be employed. One approach would be to enrich in selective fashion
the environment of a relatively deprived group of infants, such as might
be found in an institutional setting. The rate of development of such a
group could then be compared with that of a similar group not receiving
such enrichment. Under such conditions the differences might well be small,
and consequently the techniques of observation and measurement should
be as precise and as sensitive as possible to detect systematic differences.
Consequently, our first task was to determine in detail the normal sequence
of behaviors relevant to prehension spanning the first six months of life.

At the end of this time, visually-directed prehension is well developed. This preliminary information would make possible the design of sensitive and accurate scales for the measurement of prehension. We could then proceed with an examination of the role of contact with the environment in the development of this capacity. In addition, we felt that a detailed normative study of prehension was an important goal in its own right and one that would help fill an important gap in the study of human growth.

Procedure. For testing, infants were brought to a secluded nursery room where lighting, temperature, and furnishings were constant from day to day. After diapering, the infant was placed in the supine position on the examination crib. We used a standard hospital crib whose sides were kept lowered to six inches above the surface of the mattress in order to facilitate observation.

The procedure consisted of 10 minutes of observation of spontaneous behavior (pretest) during which the observers remained out of view. This period was followed by a 10 minute standardized test session during which stimulus objects were used to elicit visual pursuit, prehensory, and grasping responses. On the basis of several months of pilot work, we selected a fringed, multicolored paper party toy as the stimulus object (Fig. 9) since it seemed to produce the greatest number of responses in tests of a large number of objects. This object combines a complex contour

FIG. 9 The test object for eliciting reaching responses.

field with highly contrasting orange, red, and yellow hues. We suspect that these qualities underlie the effectiveness of this stimulus. This speculation is consistent with the findings in the field of visual preferences of human infants (Berlyne 1958; Fantz 1961a and b). The infant's view of the object consists of a red and orange display, circular in form, with a diameter of about 1½ inches. He sees a dark red core, 1 inch square, surrounded by a very irregular outline. Two feathers, one red and one yellow, protrude 1 inch from the sides. We present the object to the supine infant at 3 positions for 30 seconds each. Presentations are initiated when the infant's arms were resting on the crib surface. The infant's attention is elicited by bringing the stimulus into the infant's line of sight at a distance of about 12 inches and shaking it until the infant fixates it. The infant's head is then led to the appropriate test posture (45° left, 45° right, or midline) by moving the stimulus in the necessary direction while maintaining the infant's attention with renewed shaking of the stimulus when necessary. The object is then brought quickly to within 5 inches of the bridge of the nose and held in a stationary position. Infants over 2½ months of age do not require as much cajoling, and the stimulus may be placed at 5 inches immediately. This entire procedure takes no more than 10 seconds with most infants, but occasionally it takes much more time and effort to get young subjects to respond. The order of presentation was changed from test to test. In certain cases it was necessary to vary the position of the object to determine whether a response was accurately oriented. No infant was tested if he was ill, drowsy, asleep, or obviously distressed (Escalona 1962; Wolff 1959). On the average, each infant was tested at weekly intervals. Generally, two observers were present during testing. However, both testing and recording could be handled by a single person.

RESULTS

THE NORMATIVE SEQUENCE

We found that under our test conditions infants exhibit a relatively orderly developmental sequence which culminates in visually-directed reaching. The following outline, based on a frequency analysis, describes briefly the spontaneous behaviors and test responses characteristic for each half month interval from one through five months.

1. 1 to 1½ Months

Pretest observations. The infant lies in the tonic neck reflex position so that his head is fully turned to the side (Fig. 3). The hand toward which the eyes are oriented is often in the center of the visual field, but the eyes neither converge on it nor do they adjust to variations in its position. The infant maintains one direction of gaze for prolonged periods. The infant can be made to track a moving object with his head and eyes over an arch of 180° given the proper stimulus conditions. We have obtained reliable responses using a 7½ inch bright red circle against a 14 by 12 inch flat white background as a stimulus (Fig. 3). This target is brought into the line of sight of the supine infant at a distance of 12 to 36 inches from the bridge of his nose. Optimal distance at this age is about 24 inches. Attention is elicited by low amplitude, rapid oscillation of the stimulus in the peripheral portion of the visual field. The same motion in the foveal area is ineffective in initiating fixation. Visual pursuit is then induced by moving the target at an approximate speed of 12 inches per second in a semicircular path above the infant's head and in front of his eyes. At this age, pursuit consists of a series of jerky fixations of the red circle which bring its image to the foveal area. As the target continues to move across the field, there is a lag in the following response of the eye until the image again falls on the peripheral region of the retina. At this point, the infant responds with a rapid recentralizing of the image. If the target does not continue its motion or is moving too slowly, and therefore remains in the foveal range for more than a few seconds, the infant's gaze drifts off. We have called this level of response "peripheral pursuit."

Retinoscopic studies (Haynes, White, and Held 1965) indicate that infants have not yet developed flexible accommodative capacities at this age: their focal distance when attending to stimuli between six and sixteen inches appears to be fixed at about nine inches. Visual stimuli closer than seven inches are rarely fixated.

Test responses. In view of the foregoing retinoscopic finding, it is not surprising that the test object fails to elicit the infant's attention. Since the infant's fixed focal distance to near stimuli is approximately nine inches, the test object at five inches produces a badly blurred image on the retina. Usually, however, the infant looks away from the stimulus at this time. When he does attend to the object, he is considerably far-sighted (at least three diopters) according to retinoscopic responses. It is clear then that, during this age period, the stimulus is not as effective as it is for older infants whose accommodative capacities are more advanced. This ineffectiveness is probably attributable in large part to loss of the complexity of patterning of the retinal image caused by poor focusing. Occasionally, a brief glance may be directed at the stimulus when it is presented on the side favored by the tonic neck reflex. Presentations on the other side are most always ineffective, since they are generally outside of the infant's field of view, as a result of the tonic neck reflex.

2. 1½ to 2 Months

Pretest observations. The tonic neck reflex is typically present. The infant's eyes occasionally converge on and fixate his own hand (usually the extended hand in the preferred tonic neck reflex posture, Fig. 2). The direction of gaze now shifts occasionally to various parts of the visual surround. The responses to the retinoscope indicate that the infant now has the capacity to focus a clear image on the retina when the stimulus is six inches above the bridge of the nose. Often, at this age, a new form of visual pursuit is seen. Attention may be elicited in the foveal region using the previously described technique, and tracking is continuous over wide sectors (up to

90°) of the stimulus path. During these periods the response seems to anticipate the motion of the stimulus rather than lag behind as in peripheral pursuit. We have called this behavior "central" pursuit. This finding is in agreement with Gesell's observations (1949).

Test responses. The infant glances at the test object in all presentations. However, sustained fixations are only present on the side of the favored tonic neck reflex. At best, fixation lasts only five to ten seconds. Fixation is judged according to Ling's criteria (1942). As Wolff has noted (1960), shifts in activity level occur during these periods. At this time such shifts do not follow immediately upon fixation of the object, but appear gradually. Whether the infant becomes more or less active depends on his initial level of behavior. If an infant is alert and inactive, he usually becomes active; whereas if he is active, he becomes less so as he directs his gaze at the stimulus. The latter phenomenon is more common.

3. *2 to 2½ Months*

Pretest observations. The tonic neck reflex is still typically present although the head is now only half turned (45°) to the side. In contrast to the previous stages, the infant may shift his gaze rapidly from one part of his surround to another, and he rotates his head with comparative ease and rapidity. He now shows a good deal of interest in the examiner. The hand in view in the tonic neck reflex posture is now the object of his attention much of the time that he is awake and alert. The viewed hand may be on the crib surface or held aloft. His eyes now occasionally converge on objects as near as five inches from his eyes, and central pursuit is usually present. For the first time it is possible to elicit central pursuit of the test object placed as near as five inches and moving with a velocity of about twelve inches per second.

Test responses. Typically, the infant exhibits immediate and prolonged interest in the stimulus, fixates the object, shifts his activity level, and makes a swift, accurate swipe with the near hand. Usually the object is struck, but there is no attempt to grasp since the hand is typically fisted. The probability of a swipe response is greater when the test object is presented on the side of the commonly viewed hand which is the hand extended in the favored tonic neck reflex position.

4. *2½ to 3 Months*

Pretest observations. The tonic neck reflex is often present, though less frequently than in earlier periods. The head is often near the midline position, and the limbs are usually symmetrically placed. Sustained hand regard continues to be very common. Sustained convergence upon objects as near as three inches from the eyes can now be elicited. The infant is more active than at earlier ages. According to retinoscopic examinations, the infant's accommodative capacities are fast approaching adult standards. They differ from the adult in that there is a slightly smaller range of accurate function (five to twenty inches) and a slower rate of adaptation to the changing stimulus distances.

Test responses. All presentations of the test object result in immediate fixation and an abrupt decrease in activity. Side presentations elicit either swiping behavior as described in the previous age range or else the infant raises the near hand to within an inch or so of the object (unilateral hand raising, Fig. 10) and glances repeatedly from object to hand and back (alternating glances).

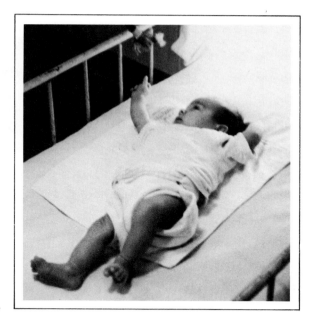

FIG. 10 Unilateral hand raising.

5. 3 to 3½ Months

Pretest observations. The tonic neck reflex is now rare, and the head is mostly at the midline position. Sustained hand regard is very common, and bilateral arm activity is more frequent than in previous months, with hands clasped together over the midline often present. Occasionally, the glance is directed toward the hands as they approach each other or during their mutual tactual exploration. The infant's accommodative performance is now indistinguishable from that of an adult.

Test responses. The typical response to a side presentation is one or both hands raised with alternating glances from the stimulus to the hand nearest the object. The middle presentation is more likely to elicit bilateral activity such as hands over the midline and clasped, or both hands up (Fig. 11), or one hand up and the other to the midline where it clutches the clothing. Here, too, alternation of glance from hand to object is common.

6. 3½ to 4 Months

Pretest observations. The tonic neck reflex is now absent. Occasional sustained hand regard continues. A common response is hands clasped over the midline, and visual monitoring of their approach and subsequent interplay are usually present.

Test responses. The responses are similar to those of the previous group with bilateral responses predominating. Hands to the midline and clasped is a favored response at this time even to a side presentation. It is now sometimes combined with a turning of the torso toward the test object (torso orienting).

7. 4 to 4½ Months

Pretest observations. Sustained hand regard is now less common, although examina-

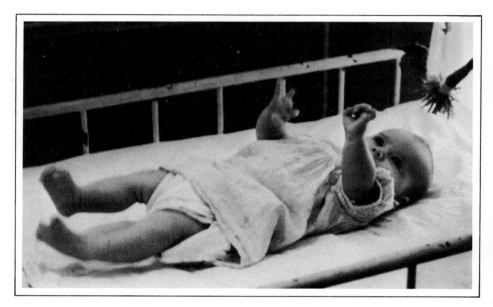

FIG. 11 Bilateral hand raising.

tion of hands clasped at the midline is sometimes present. The infant is much more active. The feet are often elevated, and the body is occasionally rotated to the side.

Test responses. Bilateral responses such as hands to midline, both hands up, or one hand up and the other to the midline are now the most common responses to all presentations. These responses are usually accompanied by several alternating glances from the stimulus to one or both hands and back to the stimulus. Torso orientation to the side presentation is now common. At times, the clasped hands are raised and oriented towards the stimulus (Fig. 12). Occasionally, one hand will be raised, looked at, and brought slowly to the stimulus while the glance shifts from hand to object repeatedly. When the hand encounters the object it is fumbled at and crudely grasped. This pattern has been described by Piaget (1952). Toward the end of this stage, opening of the hand in anticipation of contact with the object is seen.

8. 4½ to 5 Months

Pretest observations. At this age pretest findings are no different from those obtained during the previous state.

Test responses. The last stage of this sequence is signified by the appearance of what we call top level reaching.[5] This response is a rapid lifting of one hand from out of the visual field to the object. As the hand approaches the object, it opens in anticipa-

---

[5] Halverson (1932) has described the gradual refinement of visually-directed reaching from this point on. Subsequent developments, however, concern modifications of the trajectory and posture of the hand rather than new categories of prehensile response.

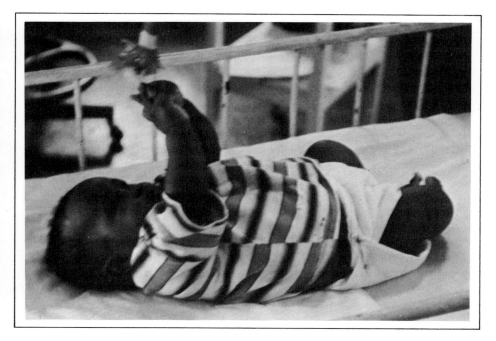

FIG. 12 Oriented hands clasped at midline.

tion of contact. Hands to the midline with alternating glances and Piaget-type responses are still more likely than top level reaching, but within the next few weeks they drop out rather quickly.

DISCUSSION

The chronology of 10 response patterns is presented in Figure 13. This chronology focuses on the test responses seen most consistently in our subject groups. The columns "Tested" and "Showing Response" indicate that some of the responses are not shown by all subjects. Although 34 subjects were tested, the group size for each response is considerably smaller for several reasons. First, infants were not available for study for a uniform period of time. All of our subjects were born at the maternity section of the hospital. Usually they were transferred to the children's section at one month of age where they remained until they were placed in private homes. Aside from neonatal screening procedures, all tests and observations were performed at the children's section. Some infants arrived from maternity at one month of age and stayed through the next five or six months. Others arrived at the same age and left after a few weeks, and still others arrived as late as 3 months of age, etc. Since we were concerned with the time of emergence of the new forms of behavior, we were obliged to exclude a large number of data because we could not be sure that a late-arriving

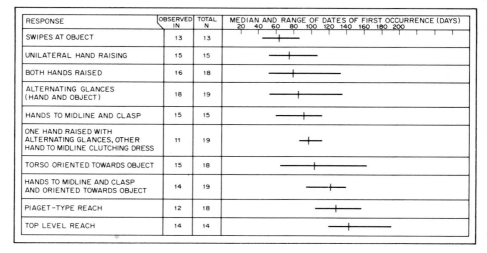

RESPONSE	OBSERVED IN	TOTAL N	MEDIAN AND RANGE OF DATES OF FIRST OCCURRENCE (DAYS)
SWIPES AT OBJECT	13	13	
UNILATERAL HAND RAISING	15	15	
BOTH HANDS RAISED	16	18	
ALTERNATING GLANCES (HAND AND OBJECT)	18	19	
HANDS TO MIDLINE AND CLASP	15	15	
ONE HAND RAISED WITH ALTERNATING GLANCES, OTHER HAND TO MIDLINE CLUTCHING DRESS	11	19	
TORSO ORIENTED TOWARDS OBJECT	15	18	
HANDS TO MIDLINE AND CLASP AND ORIENTED TOWARDS OBJECT	14	19	
PIAGET-TYPE REACH	12	18	
TOP LEVEL REACH	14	14	

FIG. 13 Normative data on the development of visually directed reaching. These data were compiled by combining the scores of control and handled infants (which did not differ significantly).

infant would not have shown the response had we been able to test him earlier.

Another factor which guided us in the analysis of our test protocols was the ease of detection of responses. Each of the 10 items listed is relatively easy to pick out of the diverse behaviors shown by infants and therefore can serve as a developmental index. At times, the presence of a response was questionable. Such data were excluded from the analysis. It is likely, therefore, that the correct median dates are actually a few days earlier than those charted. A single clear instance of a response was considered sufficient for inclusion in the "observed" column, although multiple instances were by far more common. Another relevant consideration is the limiting effect of weekly testing. Although more frequent testing would have resulted in more accurate data, we felt the added exposure to test conditions might introduce practice effects into our subject groups.

SUMMARY OF THE NORMATIVE SEQUENCE

In summary, then, given the proper object in the proper location and provided that the state of the subject is suitable, our subjects first exhibited object-oriented arm movements at about two months of age. The swiping behavior of this stage, though accurate, is not accompanied by attempts at grasping the object; the hand remains fisted throughout the response. From three to four months of age, unilateral arm approaches decrease in favor of bilateral patterns, with hands to the midline and clasped the most common response. Unilateral responses reappear at about four months, but the hand is no longer fisted and is not typically brought directly to the object. Rather, the open hand is raised to the vicinity of the object and then brought closer to it as the infant shifts his glance repeatedly from hand to object until the object is crudely grasped. Finally, just prior to five months of age, infants begin to reach for and successfully grasp the test objects in one quick, direct motion of the hand from out of the visual field.

AN ANALYSIS OF THE NORMATIVE SEQUENCE

When one examines the course of development of prehension, it becomes apparent that a number of relatively distinct sensorimotor systems contribute to its growth. These include the visual-motor systems of eye-arm and eye-hand, as well as the tactual-motor system of the hands. These systems seem to develop at different times, partly as a result of varying histories of exposure, and may remain in relative isolation from one another. During the development of prehension these various systems gradually become coordinated into a complex superordinate system which integrates their separate capacities.

During stages one and two (one to two months), the infant displays several response capacities that are relevant to the ontogeny of prehension. The jerky but coordinated head and eye movements which are seen in *peripheral* visual pursuit are one such capacity. This form of pursuit is an innate coordination since it is present at birth (Wolff and White 1965). However, another form of pursuit is seen during the second month. The smooth tracking response present in *central* visual pursuit is a more highly refined visual-motor coordination. The path now followed by the eyes appears to anticipate, and thus predict, the future position of a moving target. Whether this response is in fact predictive at this early age remains to be conclusively determined. But this growing capacity of the infant to localize and follow with both his eyes and head is clearly an important prerequisite for the development of visually-directed prehension. It should be noted that motion seems to be the stimulus property critical for eliciting attention during this stage.

Arm movements show little organized development at this stage and are limited in the variety of positions that they can assume, in large part because of the influence of the tonic neck reflex. The grasp reflex is present and can be elicited if the palm of the hand encounters a suitable object. But neither of these capacities is yet integrated with the more highly developed visual-motor tracking capacity. Infants of this age do not readily attend to near objects, namely those less than nine inches distant. Thus, it is not surprising that objects which the infant is able to explore tactually, including his own hands, are not yet visually significant. At this stage, the tactual-motor capacities of the hands remain isolated from the visual-motor ones of the eye and head.

During stages three and four (two to three months), the isolation of response capacities begins to break down, in part because the infant's eyes can now readily converge and focus on objects that are potentially within his reach. Central pursuit can be elicited from as near as five inches. One important consequence of this is that the infant now spends a good deal of time looking at his own hands. In addition, visual interest, sustained fixation, and related shifts in activity level are now readily elicited by a static presentation of the proper stimulus object. This indicates a growing capacity for focusing attention which is no longer exclusively dependent on motion.

In keeping with the above developments, it is at this stage that we see swiping, the first prehensory behavior. The appearance of this behavior indicates the development of a new visual-motor localizing capacity, one which now coordinates not only movements of the eyes and head but also those of the arms. Swiping is highly accurate, although it occasionally overshoots the target. It does not include any attempt at visually controlled grasping. Such grasping would indicate anticipation of contact with the object and is not seen at this stage. Instead, grasping is exclusively a tactually-directed pattern, which remains to be integrated into the growing visual-motor organization of prehension.

The next prehensory response, which develops soon after swiping, is that of raising a hand to within an inch or so of the stationary object followed by a series of alternating glances from object to hand and back. The crude but direct swiping response has been replaced by a more refined behavior. The visual-motor systems of eye-object and eye-hand are now juxtaposed by the infant and seem to be successively compared with each other in some way. This is the kind of behavior that Piaget refers to as the mutual assimilation and accommodation of sensorimotor schemas (1952).

During stages five and six (three to four months), the infant exhibits mutual grasping, a new pattern of spontaneous behavior. This pattern, in which the hands begin to contact and manipulate each other, is particularly important for tactual-motor development. In addition, the visual monitoring of this pattern results in the linking of vision and touch by means of a double feedback system. For the eyes not only see what the hands feel, namely each other, but each hand simultaneously touches and is being actively touched.

In keeping with these developments, hands to midline and clasped is now seen as a test response. This is a tactual-motor response pattern during which the infant fixates the object while the hands grasp each other at the midline. Grasping is thus coming to be related to the now highly developed visual-motor coordination of the head and eyes. At this time, however, grasping is not yet directed toward the external object but remains centered on the tactual interaction of the infant's own hands.

During stages seven and eight (four to five months), the infant finally succeeds in integrating the various patterns of response that have developed and coordinating them via their intersection at the object. Thus, alternating glances now become combined with the slow moving of the hand directly to the object which is fumbled at and slowly grasped. The visual-motor schemas of eye-hand and eye-object have now become integrated with the tactual-motor schema of the hand, resulting in the beginnings of visually-directed grasping. This pattern has been described by Piaget (1952). It is not until the attainment of the highest level of reaching at the end of this stage, however, that one sees the complete integration of the anticipatory grasp into a rapid and direct reach from out of the visual field. Here all the isolated or semi-isolated components of prehensory development come together in the attainment of adult-like reaching just prior to five months of age.

Increasing interest in the vision of newborn infants is demonstrated by the growing amount of research on their acuity, form discrimination, preferences, and other visually controlled behaviors (Gorman, Cogan, and Gellis 1957; Stechler 1964; Hershenson 1964; Dayton et al. 1964). In all such studies the focus of the retinal image limits the fineness of discrimination. Moreover, changes in focus may be confounded with other conditions that determine responses to visible objects. Nevertheless, in practically all research on infant vision, focal length has been an uncontrolled variable. Whereas accommodation of the lens in the eye of the young adult automatically focuses the retinal image for target distances ranging from ten cm to optical infinity, we cannot assume comparable behavior in very young infants. The fragmentary data that are available suggest limited accommodative capacity, at best, in the newborn human (Slataper 1950; Duke-Elder 1949; Feldman 1920). Even if an infant's eyes are oriented toward a target, his optical system may be focused for any distance along his line of sight. The blurring of the retinal image that results from inadequate focusing may interact significantly with the effects of experimental variables. We now report the first data known to us on the course of acquisition of accommodative ability in human infants.

Changes in accommodation are largely accomplished by involuntary contraction or relaxation of the ciliary muscle which in turn changes the shape of the crystalline lens. Retinoscopic studies performed with the ciliary muscle immobilized by atropine (cycloplegia) have suggested that the normal infant is hyperopic (farsighted) for all target distances (Slataper 1950; Duke-Elder 1949). On the other hand, Elschnig found a significant difference between responses measured during cycloplegia as opposed to nondrugged conditions in two-day-old infants (Feldman 1920). He concluded that the newborn infant is capable of some degree of accommodation. Aside from these reports we know of no others on dynamic accommodative behavior in human infants.

Dynamic retinoscopy is a technique for measuring accommodative responses without immobilizing the lenticular system (Pascal 1930; Haynes 1960). A sharply focused streak or spot of light is projected into the subject's eye through the pupillary opening. Modifications in the reflected image are used as an index of the refractive state of the eye. These mod-

---

[6] I am indebted to my colleagues, Drs. Haynes and Held, for much of the material in this section.

ifications are quantitatively assessed by means of lenses of known power. Refraction is measured while the subject fixates nearby objects and also while he tracks an object moving toward and away from his eye. Although this technique has been employed with considerable success with adults, it has been less useful with children because it requires a cooperative subject. Children of one or two years of age can rarely be induced to attend persistently to a prescribed target. Fortunately, we have found that infants between two and five months of age make good subjects for this task. Unlike older children, they will stare at appropriate targets steadily enough to allow measurement. In fact, by occasionally moving the target one can often induce the young infant to maintain fixation for several minutes. This type of performance is not at all unusual in infants during the first half year of life. Both McGraw (1943) and Ling (1942) have cited several instances of comparable "stimulus-bound" behavior in such subjects.

A white cardboard shield, 11.4 by 13.3 cm, was mounted on a Reid streak retinoscope to shield the major portion of the examiner's head from the infant's view. A 0.95 cm hole was cut in the center to allow the beam of the retinoscope to shine into the subject's eyes. Centered around this aperture, a red annulus with an outside diameter of 3.8 cm was painted. Black marks and dots were inked into this red area in a random manner to increase the complexity of the stimulus.

The study was performed on 22 infants ranging in age from 6 days to 4 months. Their time at the institution varied as a consequence of several factors, including adoption. Consequently, some subjects were available for examination only once, whereas others were tested repeatedly for several months. On the average, each subject was tested 5 times. Sample size for the 4 months varied from 7 to 13 (Fig. 14a and b). The children were examined in a supine position under standardized conditions. One examiner did the retinoscopy while the other measured the distance between the retinoscope target and the eye of the infant. To assure "on axis" retinoscopy (Pascal 1930; Haynes 1960), both examiners had to agree that the child appeared to be fixating within the 3.2 cm target area before an observation was acceptable.

The examination procedure was as follows: To capture the infant's attention, the retinoscope and attached target were moved back and forth horizontally at approximately 2.5 cm per second across the infant's line of sight. The examiner did not place his eye to the retinoscope until after pursuit fixations were obtained from at least one eye. (Infants less than 1 month of age did not exhibit sustained fixations on the target. With these subjects the examiner simply placed the retinoscope at several points along the line of gaze.) Retinoscopic measurements were taken whenever possible within each of four ranges of distance: (1) 8 to 15 cm; (2) 15 to

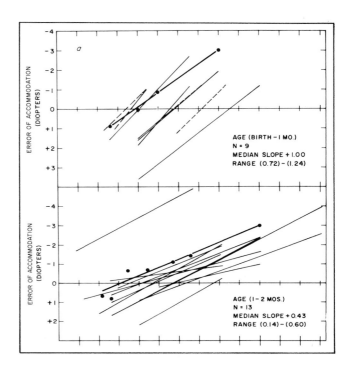

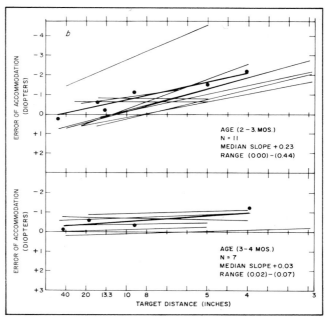

FIG. 14 Four stages in the development of accommodation in the first 4 months of life.

25 cm; (3) 25 to 51 cm; and (4) 51 to 100 cm. The typical sequence of testing was (3)-(2)-(1)-(4). The accommodative response was measured by briefly introducing lenses of known power in front of the fixating eye. By moving the retinoscope in depth, thereby inducing accommodative tracking, we then determined the range of distance over which each infant could maintain accommodation on the target within 0.5 diopter. In subjects who had developed convergence responses prior to testing, each eye was observed alternately. For each distance the average response was recorded. Since the examiner's eye was not placed exactly at the plane of the target, the data were corrected for the resultant error, as described previously (Pascal 1930; Haynes 1960). Repeated measurements were taken routinely on many of the infants. They rarely varied more than 0.5 diopter. Whenever an infant had been examined more than once in a particular month, measurements taken at replicated distances were averaged.

The corrected and averaged data for the multiple-distance retinoscopy taken during each of the 4 months were plotted for each infant. The best fitting straight line was then drawn for each subject (see Fig. 14a and b). Each line typically represents 6 points compiled from these separate examinations. The extent of the lines indicates the range of distance over which data were actually collected. The lines do not always extend over the full range, since subjects less than 2 months of age often turned away from the target when it was presented nearer than 10 cm to or farther than 38 cm from the eye. A slope value was calculated for each subject at each test age. Median slope values and their ranges were then calculated from the group data for each month starting at birth and ending at 4 months of age. The group performance for each month is shown in Figure 14a and b.

Perfect adjustment to changing target distance would be represented by a slope of 0.00, whereas the complete absence of accommodative change would be indicated by a value of ±1.00. Prior to 1 month of age, the infant's accommodative response did not adjust to changes in target distances. The system appeared to be locked at one focal distance whose median value for the group was 19 cm. This is indicated by a slope value for the group of ±1.00. Occasionally, infants of this age did not remain alert long enough to allow complete calibration of their responses. In these few instances, the magnitude of error was estimated (see Fig. 14a and b). Flexibility of response began at about the middle of the second month and performance comparable to that of the normal adult was attained by the fourth month, as shown by a median slope value of 0.03.

For infants less than 1 month of age it might be assumed that the accommodative system is incapable of any change whatever. We therefore tested 11 sleeping infants, opening their lids in order to take readings.

In every case, the lenticular system was relaxed and measured on the average 5 diopters less than when the infant was awake and alert.

During the second month of infancy, the accommodative system began to respond adaptively to change in target distance. By 3 months of age, the median magnitude of hyperopia for targets at 20 cm was 0.75 diopter, a degree of accuracy comparable to the emmetropic (normal) adult. By the time the infants began to look at their own hands and make swiping motions at nearby objects (White, Castle, and Held 1964), their eyes were able to focus sharply on such targets.

Figure 15 represents the results of a replication study on the development of visual accommodation. The data were gathered as part of the inter-observer reliability study cited earlier. Each subject was tested by two examiners (Zolot and White). The average of the two readings was the basis for the plotted curves. As in Figure 14a and b, the statistic used is an index of the flexibility of the accommodative system (the slope' of the individual's performance curve plotted at various distances over the accommodative range). The newer data are generally similar to the original, although there appears to be somewhat more flexibility in the first two months in the replication data.

FIG. 15 The development of visual accommodation—replication study.

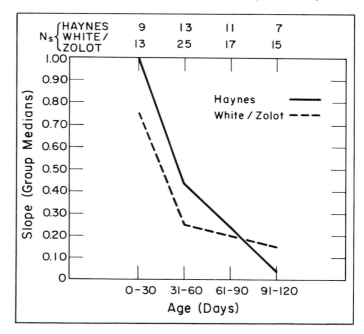

Knowledge of the developmental state of the accommodative system is a prerequisite for measuring the limits of visual discrimination in infants, because resolution is limited by the sharpness of the retinal image. Although accurate accommodation is a first step in achieving clear vision, there is not a simple relation between the capacity to focus an image on the retina and the ability to see clearly (visual acuity). Even when the image is optically focused on the retina, visual acuity in the infant is unlikely to be equivalent to that of the adult until the visual receptor mechanisms and neural pathways are sufficiently mature.

The blink response to an approaching visible target

Objective recording of the eyeblink (palpebral) response of human subjects has been accomplished in several ways. Techniques utilized have included mechanical (Brackbill 1962), magnetic (Lintz 1966), and polygraphic (Bitterman 1945) devices. Human infants make difficult subjects for such studies for several reasons. First because of the assumed vulnerability of infants, the experimenter is obliged to use unquestionably innocuous procedures. Second, the length of time necessary for the test must be brief because young infants are not awake for long periods of time. Third, there are mechanical problems caused by the infants' small size and occasional uncontrolled mobility. We have designed an apparatus appropriate for eliciting and recording blink responses from human infants 3 to 21 weeks of age.

The stimulus apparatus. The stimulating device consists of a chamber adapted to a conventional hospital crib with a target mounted above it (see Fig. 4). The interior of the chamber has been designed to orient the subject's gaze toward the target, visible through a clear plexiglass window about ½ inch above his nose. The chamber is indirectly illuminated with two shielded GE 40 watt 115–125 v lumiline bulbs (13.27 foot-candles).[7] The light inside the chamber is brighter than the room light (1.31 foot-candles), further minimizing visual diversion. The target is a 6½ inch translucent white bull's eye disc with concentric ¼ inch red rings. It is mounted on a shaft (calibrated in inches) directly above the subject's nose, and may be dropped a total distance of from 2 to 12 inches. Changes in stimulus travel may be accomplished rapidly by the shifting of an adjustable stop (see Fig. 5). The "bottoming" of the target occurs at the plexiglass shield about 1 inch from the subject's eyes, and is virtually soundless through dashpot action (see Fig. 5). The dashpot provides a noiseless

---

[7] Light levels were measured with a MacBeth Illuminometer. They should be treated as approximate values.

cushion for the stimulus, while maintaining the appearance of an abrupt cessation of motion. Target brightness level (16.28 foot-candles, white surfaces) throughout the stimulus drop has been approximately equalized by backlighting. Changes in air pressure on the subject's face are precluded by the clear plexiglass shield.

The recording system. The apparatus used for recording the blink response is a Schwarzer physioscript (PEE 4) recorder. There are two AC channels in use, as well as a time marker indicating seconds. One channel records the output from the infant, the second records stimulus action (see Fig. 7). The major electrode is placed just under the supraorbital ridge approximately 2 to 4 millimeters medial of center. The negative electrode is positioned above the zygomatic arch, in order to reduce interference from sucking and other fascio-muscular activities. The ground electrode is placed behind the opposite ear. Microswitches at the beginning and end of the target travel (see Fig. 5) register the onset and the cessation of the stimulus motion. The paper is run at a speed of 50 mm per second in order to allow an accurate assessment of temporal relationships between stimulus and response.

The procedure. The preparation of the infant for the apparatus consists essentially of securing the electrodes. It is necessary to be sure that it is primarily eyeblink being transmitted and not a conglomerate of eyeblink, eye movement, sucking, or other miscellaneous signals. A stockinette cap through which the electrodes are threaded (see Fig. 6) serves to minimize annoyance to the infant. The child is less irritated by a generalized stimulation on his head (the encircling cap) than by several discrete electrodes. Once the cap is in place, skin contact is made with conventional electrode paste and the electrodes are secured with tape. We use Johnson & Johnson air vent plastic tape for the major electrode, with either 3M Blenderm First Aid tape or 3M paper tape for the others. This procedure usually causes little resistance on the part of the child, and any restiveness can generally be overcome with an ordinary pacifier. The modification of Bitterman's placement of the electrodes which has proven most appropriate for infant work is seen in Figure 6. The child's head motions are restricted somewhat by a head rest (see Fig. 6). He is then slid supine into the chamber. The infant is positioned with the tip of his nose about ½ inch beneath the clear plexiglass shield (see Fig. 4) through which he can see the target. With his head somewhat restricted and with the target directly overhead, most infants become interested in and attend readily to the target.

The eliciting of the blink response is initiated by dropping the target from predetermined heights. For control trials, we have designed a white translucent plexiglass shield which fits over the clear window thereby obscuring the infant's view of the stimulus (see insert Fig. 4). A series of

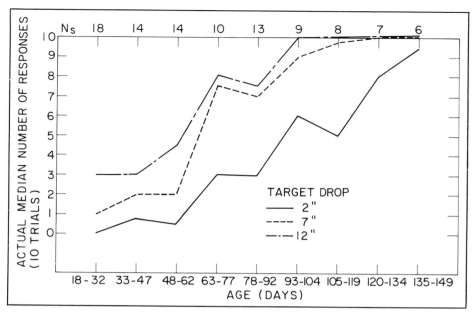

FIG. 16 Frequency of blink responses as a function of length of target drop—normative group.

FIG. 17 Latency of blink responses as a function of length of target drop—normative group.

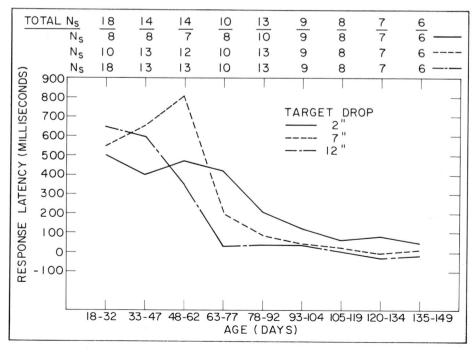

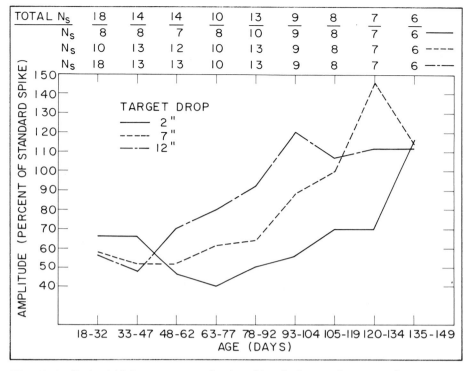

FIG. 18   Amplitude of blink responses as a function of length of target drop—normative group.

FIG. 19   Spontaneous blink rate—experimental and control groups—combined performance.

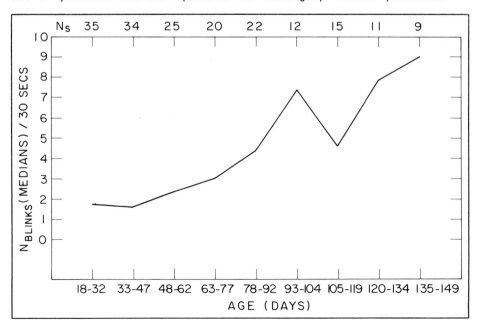

trials is then performed with the infant unable to see the target. This situation is used as a control against sounds, vibrations, or other nonvisual factors which might be either partially or solely responsible for responses in the test situation. Our entire test procedure involving 40 trials, baseline periods, placement, and removal of electrodes takes from 15 to 20 minutes and is well tolerated by nearly all subjects.

The blink apparatus as described has proved successful for testing infants ranging in age from 21 to 147 days. Even very young infants (our youngest has been 18 days) usually attend steadily to the target. As the subjects become older they often become enthusiastic, laughing and vocalizing between trials. The testing procedure itself consists initially of a calibration period, in which the child is subjected to light air puffs on the corneal surface to elicit blink responses, in order to determine the magnitude of the infants' output. Once a suitable magnitude of response has been established, a one minute record of spontaneous eyelid activity is run. The test trials consist of 10 drops from each of three heights, as well as 10 drops in the previously mentioned shielded (control) situation. The target is dropped from 12, 7, and 2 inches, the shielded drop also from a height of 12 inches. The order in which the trials are presented is vareid and is randomly selected. After the 3 test runs and 1 control series, another 1 minute baseline record is taken.

The only difficulty encountered with the procedure concerns the major electrode placement. The younger the subject, the more the likelihood of difficulty in achieving a good contact for several reasons. Infants less than 60 days old often have significant oedema round the eye which interferes with the obtaining of a clear record. A child who is initially active presents difficulties in accurate placement, but this problem can ordinarily be reduced by the introduction of a pacifier. A small baby presents a mechanical problem in terms of space available for the major electrode. Occasionally, an active baby will dislodge an electrode, or the leads may be caught by a flailing hand.

In general, the procedure seems to be efficient and useful in terms of infant tolerance, length of time involved, and ease and reliability of data collection. Acceptable records can be expected 80 to 90 per cent of the time (see Fig. 7).

Data on the development of this response are presented in Figures 16 to 19 and in Table 2.

Sensorimotor intelligence

As I have indicated earlier, Piaget's work on this topic seems unchallenged. It represents the work of a truly remarkable observer, theoretician, and experimenter and is one of the few examples of behavioral research on a grand scale. Actually, the approach Piaget used is more familiar to biologists and ethologists than to psychologists. Defining intelligence as the prime human adaptive tool, Piaget traced the ontogenesis of this vital asset from its first manifestations in the sensorimotor behavior of the newborn to the emergence of ideational forms at the end of the second year. He did this using a combination of fundamental scientific tools: (1) selection of the general topic, the development of intelligence; (2) general theorizing, e.g., the developing organism makes continuous efforts toward adaptation involving assimilation, accommodation, and schemas; (3) observations, thousands of hours spent identifying the multiplicity of manifestations of the processes under study; (4) experimentation, e.g., on object permanence, means-ends behavior, etc.; (5) refinement and integration of the theory.

Along the way, Piaget identified behavioral signs of the emergence of several related fundamental processes such as: intentionality, curiosity, symbolic behavior, etc. It is truly amazing that virtually no one (Charlesworth 1963, 1966 excepted) has pursued subsequently the study of these processes in infants, although it has been 30 years since Piaget's observations were published.

When one describes this work, one gets a feeling of remoteness from modern American studies. There is no mention of independent variables, operational definitions, elaborate experimental design, nonparametric statistics, etc., nor their counterparts of the 1930s. Yet, neither is there a feeling of artificiality, arbitrariness, and atomism characteristic of modern studies. Perhaps the most unique contribution Piaget has made to the study of infancy is to suggest a viable alternative to the conventional approach used in our field. His is the only system based on empirical evidence which addresses the question, "What does the human child know of the world during his first two years of life?"

He offers a powerful framework for guidance in investigating human behavior, a framework which is sufficiently complicated for the obviously complex creature involved, and one which pulls together the many pieces of infant behavior into a believable system. I never cease to be amazed at how often our own observations on several hundred infants confirm Piaget's observations on only three.

Perhaps the feature of Piaget's theory which attracted me the most was its focus on the intimate interaction between infant and environment. Here, after all, is where the processes that should concern psychologists take place. Even though he didn't concern himself with possible optimal arrangements of environmental circumstances or "aliments," he did open the door for anyone who would care to sponsor schema development, complication, and proliferation.

TABLE 2 NORMATIVE DEVELOPMENT OF THE BLINK RESPONSE

Age (days):	18–32	33–47	48–62	63–77	78–92	93–104	105–119	120–134	135–149
FREQUENCY [a]									
Target Drop									
2″									
N_s	18	14	14	10	13	9	8	7	6
Med	0	¾	½	3	3	6	5	8	9½
Range	0–4	0–4	0–7	0–8	0–4	3–9	1–10	3–10	5–10
7″									
N_s	18	14	14	10	13	9	8	7	6
Med	1	2	2	7½	7	9	9¾	10	10
Range	0–6	0–10	0–10	1–9	5–10	7½–10	5–10	9–10	9–10
12″									
N_s	18	14	14	10	13	9	8	7	6
Med	3	3	4½	8	7½	10	10	10	10
Range	1–6	0–10	0–10	3–10	5–10	9–10	3–10	7–10	10
Overall Median Score									
Across 2–7–12″	2	2	2	5	6	9	9	10	10
LATENCY									
2″									
N_s	8	8	7	8	10	9	8	7	6
Med	500	400	475	425	203	120	73	80	55
Range	340–600	−88–780	−120–760	160–1060	90–835	60–400	40–530	40–360	−5–140
7″									
N_s	10	13	12	10	13	9	8	7	6
Med	550	650	810	200	80	40	25	0	10
Range	360–1060	100–1100	90–1140	60–800	0–255	−5–120	−95–200	−30–40	−80–30

12"	N_8	18	13	13	10	13	9	8	7	6
	Med	650	600	350	35	40	40	5	-20	-15
	Range	20-1200	0-960	0-1050	0-320	-50-880	-30-80	-120-100	-60-60	-125-0
Overall Median Score Across 2-7-12"		555	640	580	250	90	60	55	30	0
AMPLITUDE										
2"	N_8	8	8	7	8	10	9	8	7	6
	Med(%)	66	66.5	47	40	51	57	70	70	116
	Range(%)	30-107	26-140	30-120	25-100	32-93	40-67	25-174	67-143	53-144
7"	N_8	10	13	12	10	13	9	8	7	6
	Med(%)	58	52	53	61	73	87	100	147	114
	Range(%)	33-136	27-130	32.5-100	25-147	36-140	40-160	35-175	80-214	67-208
12"	N_8	18	13	13	10	13	9	8	7	6
	Med(%)	56	47	70	80	93	120	106	113	113
	Range(%)	25-113	30-107	27-150	30-275	40-140	53-74	35-174	58-166	98-208
Overall Median Score Across 2-7-12"		50	60	50	67	67	65	90	105	116

[a] There were 10 randomly spaced target drops of 2, 7, and 12 inches. In all trials the target bottomed at from 1½-2 inches from the corneal surfaces of the infant's eyes.

At this point, I would like to present some data on one phase of sensori-motor theory. These data concern the integration of schemas or, in Piaget's terms, the "reciprocal coordinations" of the second stage. As a part of our prehension assessment procedures we routinely included an "object-in-hand" test. According to Piaget, the behavior seen when an object is grasped by an infant of one to five months of age reveals the degree of interrelationship among the grasp, sucking, and looking schemas. The one-month-old infant is capable of grasping a rattle, looking at it, or sucking it. Further, each of these behaviors can be elicited if the rattle is used as directed "aliment," i.e., if it is brought to the infant's mouth, he will suck it; if it is pressed in the infant's palm, he will grasp it, etc. However, for an infant of one month, according to Piaget, these schemas exist in isolation. This means that, unlike an adult, a one-month-old infant will not look at something he's grasping, nor grasp what he is sucking, etc. During the months that follow, these schemas become coordinated. The steps as spelled out by Piaget (1952, pp. 88-122) are:

1. *1–2 months.*[8]   The hand does not grasp an object which is being sucked, even though the hand itself is occasionally brought to the mouth and sucked. Further, the eyes do not regard the object grasped (or the hand). Vision is therefore not as advanced as sucking in regard to control of the hands.

2. *2–3 months.*   The eyes follow the motion of the hands but the hands are not under the control of the visual system; they move in and out of the visual field apparently independently. The hand does not try to grasp what the eye sees. Continuing the primacy of sucking as a controlling function, the hand brings grasped objects to the mouth where they are sucked rather than to the visual field for viewing.

3. *3–4 months.*   The hand grasps the object that is being sucked and, reciprocally, the object grasped is brought to the mouth to be sucked. However, if the object is in view before it is grasped, there is a delay before the object is brought to the mouth. In addition, vision seems to influence hand movements, maintaining their presence in the visual field and "augmenting" their activity (Piaget 1952, p. 102).

4. *4–5 months.*   The hand grasps the seen object for the first time. Prehension results when hand and object are simultaneously in view.

5. *5–6 months.*   True visually-directed reaching emerges. After the object is grasped, the infant routinely glances at it before bringing it to the mouth for sucking. Occasionally, viewing is prolonged, and the object is not brought to the mouth at all. It should be noted that in sensorimotor theory the intersection of several schemas provides the basis for the emergence of object permanence. An object that is simultaneously looked at, reached for, and felt, as in the prehensory act, is more than a part of a single activity schema. It serves a truly unique function when it partici-

[8] Ages cited are approximations.

pates in three schemas at once, and it is from this special role that true object permanence normally develops (Hunt 1961).

Unfortunately, placing an object in the hand of an infant is an inadequate test of the developmental sequence in question. For example, a test situation where an object (perhaps a pacifier) was placed in the infant's mouth would be necessary as well as a situation where the infant could view the object before he grasped it. Nonetheless, we may be able to learn something from this admittedly partial view of the situation when the results are combined with those of tests of prehension in the same subjects.

Procedure. Once each week, beginning at 36 days, each infant was brought to the testing room. After a 5 to 10 minute acclimatization period, the infant was given 3 opportunities to respond to the presentation of the test object. (For details see the earlier section on prehension in this chapter.) This procedure took about 5 minutes. The last phase of the session consisted of the object-in-hand test. The test object was the paper party toy used in the prehension test but, in this situation, not attached to an extension rod. It was therefore approximately 5 inches in length and ½ inch in diameter along the handle or stem. The data presented are from 43 babies, including 11 who had received extra handling during the first 36 days of life.

RESULTS

TABLE 3   THE NORMAL DEVELOPMENTAL SEQUENCES
ACCORDING TO PIAGET

Age (months)	N	Test: Object-In-Hand Response	Prehension Response
1–2	3	1. Retains only	—
2–3	3	1. Brought to mouth for sucking	—
3–4	3	1. Brought to mouth for sucking	—
4–5	3	1. Brought to mouth for sucking	Fourth stage reaching (if hand and object simultaneously in view)
5–6	3	1. Brief regard then brought to mouth for sucking 2. Prolonged regard	True reaching

Source: White (1969a). Copyright 1969 by Oxford University Press.

TABLE 4 THE SEQUENCE EXHIBITED BY CONTROL SUBJECTS

Age (months)	N [a]	Test: Object-In-Hand Response	Subjects Exhibiting N	Response % [b]	N	Prehension Response
1½–2	23	1. Retains only	22	95.8		
		2. Brought to mouth	5	21.7		
		3. Views	3	13.0		
2–2½	27	1. Retains only	23	85.2		
		2. Views other hand	3	11.1		
		3. Views–other hand raised	2	7.4		
2½–3	25	1. Retains only	21	84.1		
		2. Views	18	72.1		
		3. Brought to mouth	6	24.0		
		4. Views other hand	5	20.0		
		5. Monitored mutual play	0	0.0		
3–3½	27	1. Views	24	89.0		
		2. Retains only	16	59.3		
		3. Monitored mutual play	7	25.9		
		4. Brought to mouth	6	22.2		
3½–4	25	1. Views	20	80.0		
		2. Monitored mutual play	13	52.0		
		3. Views then to mouth	7	28.0		
		4. Retains only	6	24.0		
		5. Brought to mouth	6	24.0		
		6. Views other hand raised	6	24.0		
		7. Monitored mutual play then to mouth	3	12.0		
4–4½	21	1. Views	17	81.0	12	4th stage reaching (median—130 days)
		2. Monitored mutual play	15	71.5		
		3. Views other hand raised	7	33.3		
4½–5	16	1. Views	12	75.0	14	True reaching (median—147 days)
		2. Monitored mutual play	9	56.3		
		3. Brought to mouth	6	37.5		
		4. Views then to mouth	6	37.5		
		5. Monitored mutual play then to mouth	1	6.3		

Source: White (1969a). Copyright 1969 by Oxford University Press.
Note: Total N = 164. Total trials = 560.
[a] Each test consisted of two trials. Average number of tests/subject was 1.71. Average number of responses per trial was 1.21, increasing steadily with age.
[b] Only responses occurring in 20% or more of the subjects of either the control or experimental group are recorded.

DISCUSSION: THE NORMAL DEVELOPMENTAL SEQUENCE

On the basis of Piaget's discussion of the development of prehension schemas (1952, pp. 88-122), one would expect a developmental pattern somewhat like that described in Table 3.

Responses to the object-in-hand test in our control group are shown in Table 4.

DESCRIPTION OF RESPONSES

1. *Retains only.* The infant holds the test object for more than three seconds.
2. *Views.* The infant holds the test object and either glances at it one or more times or regards it steadily for up to two minutes.
3. *Brought to mouth.* The infant holds the object and without viewing, brings it to the mouth one or more times briefly or manages to keep it at the mouth and gum or suck it.
4. *Monitored and mutual play.* The object is brought to the midline where it is simultaneously viewed and tactually explored by the other hand.
5. *Views then to mouth.* Responses (2) and (3) combined.
6. *Views, other hand raised.* The infant retains the object and extends and raises both arms while viewing the object.
7. *Views other hand.* The infant retains the object and views the free hand.
8. *Monitored mutual play, then to mouth.* Responses (4) and (3) combined.

Although fourth and fifth stage reaching occurred about as predicted by Piaget's work, this was not the case for the object-in-hand data. The number of response patterns seen was considerably greater than expected. The influence of the sucking schemas was much less than expected, and that of vision was strikingly greater than expected.

Piaget's general position which holds that infant behavior consists at first of sequential activation of isolated schemas and, from the third month on, their reciprocal coordination, is generally confirmed in this study. The sequences of responses described by Piaget were, however, only partly exhibited by our subjects. We did not find the sucking schema to be dominant in our subjects. Further, the influence of vision was markedly greater than expected. In addition, the complexity of the sequence in terms of number of responses shown was greater than expected. Finally, the influence of postural factors such as the tonic neck reflex and the favored hand was both marked and unexpected. During the third month of life, a child would often view the object placed in his favored hand, and again view that hand when the object was placed in the other hand. Another manifestation of this asymmetry was seen a few weeks later when the infant would merely stare at the object in the favored hand (views object) but would bring the favored hand over to join or tactually explore the object when it was held by the other hand (monitored mutual play). Responses during the second month usually involved only one hand. During the third and fourth months there was steady increase in bilateral hand and arm involvement which paralleled the oft-noted reduction in the influence of the tonic neck reflex (Gesell and Amatruda 1941). This paves the way for the coordination of the visual and tactual schemas of each hand with the other. It is of course possible that the fact that Piaget's children were breast fed, whereas the subjects in this study were not, would account for some or even all of the differences.

ETHOLOGICAL SKETCHES

To sum up this chapter, I would like to provide an ethological characterization of the normal human infant from birth to six months of age. This characterization will necessarily be incomplete because our knowledge is spotty. Further, it will not always be supported by evidence. I shall take the liberty of injecting some speculation and impressions into the description to round out the limited view provided by the bits and pieces of evidence we have. Ideally, this field ought to have a large body of carefully collected field studies of representative infant behavior available to students and researchers. It does not. The nearest we have is in the work of Gesell (Gesell and Amatruda 1941; Gesell and Ilg 1943; Gesell, Ilg, and Bullis 1949) which constitutes only a beginning. Lorenz, studying other species, can perhaps afford to relegate individual differences to a minor position because of the greater proportion of stereotyped situations and behaviors found in studies of infrahuman subjects. It is clear, however, that with respect to both situational and individual differences the first six months of human development are probably considerably more variable than the comparable developmental periods of other species. The high probability of greater diversity demands a larger investment of energies. Unfortunately, aside from a handful of baby biographies (Shinn, Preyer, and Darwin cited in Wright 1960) we have no ethologies of human development at all (a refreshing exception is Church's book 1966).

Because his rate of psychological growth is so high in the first months of life, the human infant from birth to six months of age seems best considered as not one but several types of subject. I would distinguish three stages, birth to six weeks, six weeks to three and a half months, three and a half months to six months. As we refine our knowledge, I would predict that further differentiations will be justified.[9]

---

[9] The infant less than five days of age has been by far the most popular subject in the field. This has been the case not because the first four days of life are necessarily of paramount importance, although they must of course be studied, but simply because groups of infants of that age are accessible in hospital nurseries. In this respect, the less than five-day-old infant resembles the white rat and the college sophomore. Unfortunately, the fact that one type of subject is readily available is not likely to mean that his behavior is representative of the entire population in question. Consequently, the overinvestment of research in a particular subject group brings with it the danger of inappropriate generalizations.

The newborn is a very inept creature, notwithstanding reports of precocious visual behavior (Fantz 1964). Behaviorally, there is little evidence that he is capable of a great deal of differentiated activity. True, he comes equipped with several semi-functional reflexes, such as the rooting (Praechtl), blinking (palpebral response), Babinski, sneeze, patellar, head-rearing, grasp, and startle response, but compared to the six-month-old or even the three-month-old child, he is decidedly helpless, underdeveloped, and uninteresting to observe. For one thing, his typical state is sleep or drowsiness. Wolff and I have spent hundreds of hours in protracted observations of newborns and our data are quite consistent. Figure 8 illustrates the growth of visual alertness during the first six months of life for physically normal infants reared in institutions. The data for the first few weeks of life are very probably representative of most human infants regardless of rearing (Piaget 1952; Gesell and Amatruda 1941).

In Piaget's system, this period is one in which the innate behaviors become stabilized through exercise if environmental circumstances provide appropriate stimulation. For most of the innately organized behaviors exercise is assured. The grasp, startle, and rooting responses, for example, are guaranteed the opportunity to function in the normal course of care-taking functions. How much exercise they need and what purposes they serve are obscure. Piaget claims that grasping, unlike the startle or sneeze, is a behavior of great importance for future development since it gradually develops into active or voluntary haptic exploration and, ultimately, visually-directed reaching.

Investigators familiar with infants, especially McGraw (1943), have claimed that behavior at this time is under the control of subcortical centers of the central nervous system. Infants do appear to be reactive rather than proactive organisms during this period. For example, one can elicit visual pursuit during this period (Wolff and White 1965; Dayton and Jones 1964) by shaking a large red target in the peripheral regions of the infant's visual field. Provided he is in a state of alert inactivity, he will usually centralize the object. If the target is not quickly moved again to the periphery of the field, he will soon lose interest in it, but if it is moved, he will centralize it again. A series of such *saccadic* movements constitutes visual pursuit; however, each step is a mechanical reaction in contrast to the pursuit seen in the two-month-old infant which is facile, virtually continuous, and appears to lead the target. The same pattern is true of rooting behavior which during the first three months gradually changes from a single ballistic reaction to apparently voluntary multi-stepped searchings with the mouth.

Another interesting quality of the very young infant is his tendency to startle. Wolff (1959) has studied the spontaneous and elicited startles of the newborn. He notes an inverse relation between startle and level of motor activity. A curious feature of the startle is that during the first weeks of life a wide variety of abrupt changes in stimulation will trigger the reaction. A bright flash of light, a loud noise, a sudden short drop in space, or even an abrupt tactile stimulus will almost invariably produce a startle in a resting neonate. A point to mention at this time is that the first phase of the startle response consists of the eyeblink which is then followed by abrupt arm and leg motion.

In the area of intellectual or pre-intellectual function, two facts seem clear. Infants less than six weeks old are not easily conditioned, and their primitive behavior repertoire consists of a series of reflex-like functions which appear to operate independently of each other. As to conditionability, although many have sought to demonstrate that some form of conditioning must occur routinely in the neonatal period, the clear conclusion must be that infants are not easily conditioned (Papousek and Bernstein, In Press). It is not until the end of the infant's second month of life that researchers routinely report consistent success in establishing conditioned responses and more than very short-lived learning effects. The thesis that neonates are learning a great deal and that the familiar conditioning processes are the primary modes by which such learning proceeds has not been demonstrated in spite of many vigorous attempts.

Piaget's theory of cognitive development has not yet undergone significant empirical testing. To my knowledge, the only report on early infancy which specifically addresses his ideas is one of my own (White 1969a). In that paper and in this chapter, I have reported a general confirmation of Piaget's views on schema development and pre-intellectual behavior during the first six months of life. Piaget's view is that during the first six weeks the only form of learning behavior consists of the increase in the efficacy of innate reflex-like behavior patterns such as the grasp and the rooting response. He does not concern himself with the entire innate repertoire. The sneeze and the knee jerk (patellar) are examples of behavior patterns which seem irrelevant to the development of intelligence. In addition, Piaget does not believe that the infant of this age is "intelligent" [10] but rather that the development involved in the "exercise" of such behavior as the grasp and visual pursuit is decidedly prerequiste for later truly intellectual emergents.

---

[10] Piaget's definition of intelligence involves purposeful means-ends behavior. There is no clear indication of such instrumental activity in the first weeks of life except in the sense that there is a teleologic component to all reflex-like behavior. It is only when the infant uses one behavior in the service of another, such as when he pushes aside an obstacle to prehend an object, that Piaget credits him with "intelligence."

Six weeks to three and a half months

The six week to three and a half month old infant is, on the other hand, a fascinating subject. He is increasingly more alert, active, and curious. A great many significant processes undergo dramatic change during this period. First of all the infant is alert and exploring the world for the first time in protracted fashion. It is as if the first six weeks were exclusively concerned with the physical transition from pre- to postnatal existence. He is now ready to get on with the task of developing the skills and information to deal with the external world. During this eight week period he will discover and gain at least partial mastery over the use of his hands, fully develop the capacity to maintain clear focus on objects moving nearby (visual accommodation), increase his periods of alertness from less than ten minutes per hour to almost half the daylight hours, enter into a period of social smiling guaranteed to endear him to any but the coldest of adult hearts, acquire the tendency to blink at approaching visible targets, overcome the restrictive influence of the grasp reflex which in the neonatal period kept his hands mostly fisted, overcome the influence of the tonic neck reflex which had restricted his visual range and subordinated the motions of his limbs to the position of his head, acquire the capacity to hold his head vertically for several minutes when placed prone, begin to assimilate experiences which will lead to the construction of a world of objects (himself included) (Piaget 1952), exhibit the capacity to sustain interest in a spectacle (his own hands) for up to thirty minutes at a time, begin to exhibit the ability to imitate sounds, distinguish familiar social figures, make many fine sensory discriminations, form dependable conditioned responses, etc.

This six week to three and a half month period might be characterized as the dawning of awareness and voluntary action. Though the infant ordinarily cannot locomote (except for an occasional displacement of his body most commonly seen during rage states), nor reach successfully for objects, he now appears much more at home in the postnatal world. He is awake and alert much more often (Fig. 8). Further, he now seems to examine the details of nearby visible targets. Such a subjective opinion is supported by a good deal of data. Fantz, for example, reports a preference for more complicated three dimensional forms at about two months (1961a). Our retinoscope data indicate rapid completion of the development of accommodative capacity, and visual convergence (Peiper 1963) seems to become functional as well during this period. As for volition, the child's searching movements with eyes, mouth and hands all lose their stereotyped, ballistic quality. The child's behavior (especially toward the end of this period) conveys the impression that he is less a captive of or bound by stimuli than in the first weeks. Many years ago Ling, in a study of the development of fixation responses (1942), noted an emergent capacity to exhibit a "take it or leave it" attitude toward the target at about this time.

Yet, in spite of these impressive changes, until the infant acquires the ability to use his hands to reach for and examine objects, all he can do to explore the external world is either lie on his back and stare or, if prone, he can with increasing skill raise his head and peer about.

Three and a half to six months

The crowning observable achievement of the period from three and a half to six months is visually-directed reaching. Most all six-month-old infants will reach with surprising accuracy for proffered small objects. They behave as reliably in this respect as they did when stimulated to root or startle during the first weeks of life. The regularity with which they reach for objects at this time suggests a compulsion almost as potent as that behind the patellar (knee jerk) reflex, even though a psychological as well as a physical circuit is being activated. The infant of this age is a truly delightful creature, especially during the fourth month of life. Except in the case of an infant who has been subjected to severe hardships or is ill, all babies of this age seem to be euphoric. They smile indiscriminately and often [though Ambrose (1961) has shown that the first preference for the mother appears at this time]. Further, the smile is symptomatic of a chronically positive affect tone which makes them a delight for parents, photographers, and researchers. From four to ten weeks or so, the infant is at a peak with respect to reflexive responses. The reliability at that time of the rooting, visual pursuit, blink to an approaching object, fixation, smile responses, and others is truly remarkable. In this period the reliability of the mood is no less striking.

Also at this time under certain conditions, the infant may, for the first time, manifest a good deal of curiosity and humor. As Piaget has pointed out, infants at this age will occasionally smile at familiar nonsocial objects such as their own hands, or toys, or other objects they have seen frequently. Their excitement at times grows and leads to gurgling, laughter, and other signs of hilarity. These expressions of affect usually follow periods of sustained viewing which may last as long as thirty minutes.

The infant has now become much more vigorous and competent in the control of his body. Whereas earlier he conveyed the impression of fragility, he now appears ebullient and strong. When he is held in a sitting posture, his head no longer threatens to fall from the upright position. Pressure on the soles of the feet results in a powerful extensor reflex. Given an appropriately designed object, he will strike it repeatedly and with surprising force.

Intellectually, while still not usually ready to exhibit intelligent, instrumental behavior, he is developing rapidly. A good deal of time is spent in mutual exploration of his hands, at first by touch alone, then later visually-monitored. He engages in countless interactions with his nearby environment now that he is awake and alert a good deal (Fig. 8). Piaget describes how the previously isolated action systems are being coordinated at this time. Things grasped are now looked at, things in the mouth are now touched, things heard are now looked at, etc. It is in these activities that Piaget sees the preparation for the emergence of an awareness of an object world with a separate existence. In reaching for objects under the guidance of vision, the nucleus of independent existence of objects is developed. (For a more extensive treatment of this process see Hunt 1961.)

5

RECENT ADDITIONS TO WHAT WE KNOW ABOUT THE ROLE OF EARLY EXPERIENCE

BACKGROUND OF THE STUDIES

As I've already mentioned, I'm not an advocate of elaborate theorizing in the field of infancy at this stage of development. I'm impressed by Piaget's general biological view of development as a continuing process of adaptation. I'm also impressed by his concepts of assimilation and accommodation, among others. But, Piaget's theory doesn't deal with the mechanisms of development in the moment-to-moment experiences of the child. For example, Held (1961) claims that information is processed and the infant develops only when he performs certain motor acts within certain kinds of sensory surrounds. Hunt (1961) argues that the infant's motor involvement can be restricted to the ocular and extra-ocular muscles in the first month and that more extensive motor involvement only becomes necessary later. Such discussions of mechanisms speak to a very practical level of experimental design in contrast to the concepts of assimilation and accommodation which are fairly high-level abstractions. There are other theoretical views of this problem, but I prefer to gather a more comprehensive data base and perhaps save the wasted effort of premature theorizing.

We did one handling study because there was a weight of evidence from several sources which was consistent with what we have learned about infants in the first weeks of life. Mainly, however, I prefer to assume that active involvement by the infant is the general prerequisite for development and then to concentrate on the quality of that involvement. Major clues to the types of experience to sponsor come from what we discover about emerging abilities and interests of infants. An additional assumption therefore is that "feeding" newly emerging abilities is the clue to designing the optimal "match" between infant and environment. Beyond this point, I'm not ready to go.

FIRST MODIFICATION OF REARING CONDITIONS— THE HANDLING STUDY

Several recent studies (Denenberg and Karas 1959; Levine 1957; Meier 1961) have demonstrated the profound effects of postnatal handling on the subsequent development of laboratory reared animals such as rats and kittens. These have included changes in learning capacities, exploratory behavior, emotionality, response to stress, and other behaviors. Furthermore, animals, receiving such treatment were healthier and gained weight more rapidly than controls. In general, small amounts of handling, experimentally administered early in postnatal life, have resulted in the acceleration of both overall physical development and adaptive functioning. At the time of this study only one study of the consequences of handling human infants had been reported.[1] Ourth and Brown (1961) found significantly less crying in infants to whom four hours of extra handling was administered daily during the first four and a half days of life.

In recent reviews of studies of maternal deprivation, both Yarrow (1961) and Casler (1961) conclude that early tactile stimulation appears necessary for normal human development. A related finding was reported by Brody (1951), who remarked that infants receiving moderate amounts of maternal handling seemed to be more interested in their visual surroundings than those who received minimal amounts of such stimulation. There is then suggestive evidence at least that the rather striking effects of early postnatal handling of lower animals should have analogues in human development. Would extra handling of our subjects, who normally receive minimal amounts, result in accelerated visual-motor development?

Procedure. The normal hospital procedure is such that during the first months of life the infants receive little handling. At 4-hour intervals, diapers are changed and the infants are held for a 15-minute bottle feeding. They also receive a brief sponge bath each morning, at which time they are weighed. This was the schedule under which our control group ($n = 18$)

---

[1] Since this study was performed, Casler has reported on another study of the effects of extra handling on infants (see Chapter 3).

was reared during the first month of life. This procedure was altered for an experimental group ($n = 10$). Beginning with the sixth day of life and continuing for the next 30 days, our experimental infants were given 20 minutes of extra handling daily. Nurses provided 10 minutes of handling per infant during each of the 2-hour periods midway between feedings, morning and afternoon. This period was selected for two reasons. We wanted to be quite sure that the infants would be through feeding before the experimental period began, and we also wanted to avoid the hour just prior to the next feeding time during which increasing hunger often produces choruses of piercing cries in young infants.

Assuming that some of the crying during these early weeks might indicate a need for tactual, vestibular, and kinesthetic stimulation, we adopted the following procedures: (1) As soon as an infant engaged in noticeable crying, the nurse briefly examined the child, changed cold or soiled diapers, and eliminated any other obvious sources of discomfort, such as improperly arranged bed clothes. (2) If the crying then persisted for 30 seconds or was intermittent beyond 2 minutes, the infant was removed from its crib and rocked for at least 2 minutes, or until he remained quiet for 30 seconds. He was then returned to his crib. This procedure was repeated, as necessary, until a total of 10 minutes of handling had been administered in each period. (3) If an infant had not displayed any crying during the first 1½ hour of a period and subsequently awoke, he was then rocked continuously for 10 minutes. If, however, he had not awakened by this time he was rocked continuously for 10 minutes, regardless of his state during the last 15 minutes of the 2-hour period. Handling was administered by the nurse holding the infant upright and against her breast while rocking continuously in a rocking chair. During rocking, though the infant's eyes were rarely open, they were covered with a blindfold to control for any possible increase in visual experience. This method of handling proved to be remarkably effective. In only 3 of 600 experimental periods did an infant exhibit continued signs of displeasure while being rocked. In these cases, nurses were advised to comfort the infant in any manner possible. Typically, 3 to 5 additional minutes of varied handling was sufficient for these purposes.

Measure. Testing followed the 30 days of handling for both groups who were now 37 days old. Data were gathered in several developmental areas including visual attention, prehension (visually-directed reaching), performance on the Gesell developmental schedules, rate of weight gain, and incidence of sickness. Except for the Gesell schedules, data were gathered on a weekly basis. Gesell tests were administered biweekly. A continuous 3-hour record of visual attention and motor activity was kept, starting 1 hour after feeding.

The development of prehension was assessed using procedures described

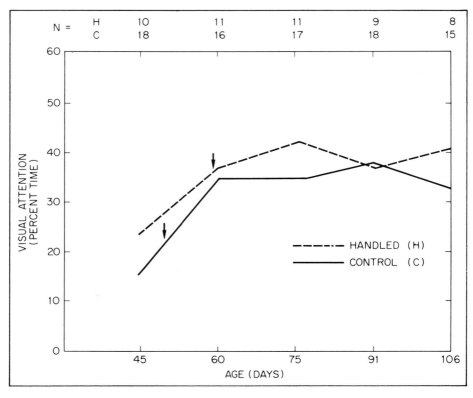

FIG. 20 Comparison of visual attention among control subjects and in those given extra handling.

elsewhere (White, Castle, and Held 1964). The rate of weight gain and incidence of sickness data were abstracted from hospital records.

No differences were found in any developmental process except the growth of visual attention. The handled group was more visually attentive than controls.[2] Note that the shapes of the curves in Figure 20 are quite similar. Sustained hand regard appeared somewhat later in the handled group (day 60) than in controls (day 49, see Table 5). Upon relocation in large, open-sided cribs the handled group, like the control group, exhibited a sharp increase in visual attentiveness.

---

[2] In a previous report (White and Castle 1964), we indicated that this increase in visual attention was statistically significant. In fact, the analysis used was somewhat inappropriate. In addition, we have added data from one new subject. Subsequent analyses (see Tables 6, 7, and 8) indicate a strong trend that fails to reach significance at the .05 level.

This study suggested that innocuous environmental modifications might alter the development of important visual-motor functions such as exploratory behavior. No evidence for comparable plasticity in other visual-motor developments was found following the extra handling. It is possible that further exploration of the effects of early handling would produce still greater increases in visual exploratory behavior.

TABLE 5   SIGNIFICANCE OF DIFFERENCES BETWEEN EXPERIMENTAL AND CONTROL GROUPS IN AGE AT ONSET OF SUSTAINED HAND REGARD

Condition (N of Ss; mdn Age in days at onset)	Handled (N = 10; mdn = 60)	Massive Enrichment (N = 14; mdn = 61)	Modified Enrichment (N = 15; mdn = 44)
Control (N = 16; mdn = 49)	.1469, NS	.0571, NS	.1867, NS
Handled (N = 10; mdn = 60)		.4168, NS	.0136
Massive Enrichment (N = 14; mdn = 61)			.0016

Source: White (1967). © 1967 University of Minnesota.

Note: Table entries are significance levels based on Mann-Whitney U (1-tailed) tests. In order to conclude that the groups compared come from significantly different (.05 level) parent populations, compensation must be made for the fact that a number of pairs have been sampled. In this case, six pairs are sampled, and the significance level must reach .008 before it can be concluded that the two groups differ. This value was derived from the following formula: $p = (1 - a)^n$, where $p = .05$, n = number of pairs compared, and a = the level of significance which must be found for any single pair in order to conclude that there is more than one parent population involved.

SECOND MODIFICATION OF REARING CONDITIONS— THE MASSIVE ENRICHMENT STUDY

Several studies seem to indicate that visual-motor performance depends to a significant extent on experience of some kind for its development. Riesen's (1958) work demonstrated that chimpanzees required exposure to patterned environment is also required for adequate development. Held and his collaborators (Held and Bossom 1961; Held 1961; Mikaelian and Held 1964) have repeatedly demonstrated the importance of self-induced movement in dependably structured environments for adaptation to rearranged sensory inputs in human adults. More recently, their study of neonatal kittens showed the applicability of these findings to developmental processes (Held and Hein 1963). The results of this study indicated that movement per se in the presence of dependable surroundings was insufficient for normal visual-motor development. Kittens whose movements were externally-produced rather than self-induced did not develop normally. Self-induced movement in dependable surroundings was found necessary for adequate development as well as for maintenance of stable visual-motor behavior.

Our subjects were usually reared under conditions that are obviously less than optimal with respect to the kinds of experience discussed above. Motility was limited by soft mattresses with depressions in them as well as by the supine posture in which these infants were kept. The visual surroundings were poorly figured. Consequently, according to our hypothesis, heightened motility in enriched surroundings should produce accelerated visual-motor development.

As a first test we enriched the environment of a group of nineteen infants in as many respects as feasible (White 1967):

1. *Increased tactual-vestibular stimulation.* Each infant received 20 minutes of extra handling each day from day 6 through day 36.

2. *Increased motility.* Infants were placed in the prone posture for 15 minutes after the 6 A.M., 10 A.M., and 2 P.M. feeding each day from day 37 through day 124. At these times, the crib liners were removed, making the ward activities visible to the child. Movements of the head and trunk in the presence of figured visual surroundings resulted from the normal tendency of infants to rear their heads under such circumstances. The crib mattresses were flattened, thereby facilitating head, arm, and trunk motility.

3. *Enriched visual surroundings.* A special stabile featuring highly contrasting colors and numerous forms against a dull white background was suspended over these infants from days 37 through 124 (see Fig. 21). In addition, printed multicolored sheets and bumpers were substituted for the standard white ones. These changes were designed to reproduce heightened visual interest and increased hand movement because of the normal tendency of infants to swipe at visible objects nearby.

Weekly measures of prehensory responses and visual attention were made. The rates of development of spontaneous behaviors related to visual-motor function such as hand regard, hands touching at the midline, mutual fingering, and turning of the torso were assessed from the records of the three-hour observation periods. Performance on the Gesell tests was recorded at bi-weekly intervals to determine general developmental progress. Also, records of rate of weight gain and general health were kept.

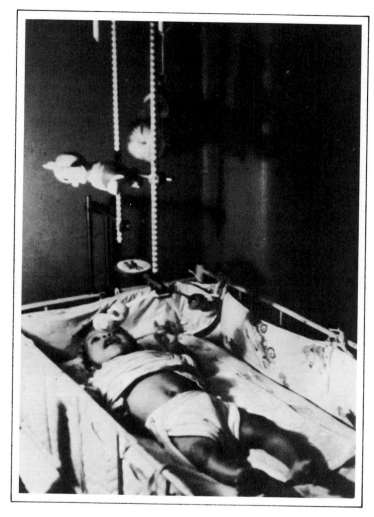

FIG. 21   The massive enrichment condition.

RESULTS

HAND REGARD AND SWIPING

Hand regard as such was much less frequently shown by this group than by controls. Instead the hands were generally first observed as they contacted portions of the experimental stabile. We called this pattern monitored stabile play and considered it together with monitored bumper play as forms of hand regard. By these criteria the onset of hand regard was delayed for some twelve days in our experimental group (see Fig. 28). The onset of swiping was also set back, but only by some five days (a nonsignificant difference). Figure 22 illustrates the responses to the test object leading to reaching for this group.

RESPONSE	OBSERVED IN	TOTAL N	MEDIAN AND RANGE OF DATES OF FIRST OCCURRENCE (DAYS)
SWIPES AT OBJECT	11	14	
UNILATERAL HAND RAISING	12	13	
BOTH HANDS RAISED	12	13	
ALTERNATING GLANCES (HAND AND OBJECT)	10	11	
HANDS TO MIDLINE AND CLASP	7	10	
ONE HAND RAISED WITH ALTERNATING GLANCES, OTHER HAND TO MIDLINE CLUTCHING DRESS	5	9	
TORSO ORIENTED TOWARDS OBJECT	4	9	
HANDS TO MIDLINE AND CLASP AND ORIENTED TOWARDS OBJECT	3	9	
PIAGET-TYPE REACH	6	9	
TOP LEVEL REACH	9	9	

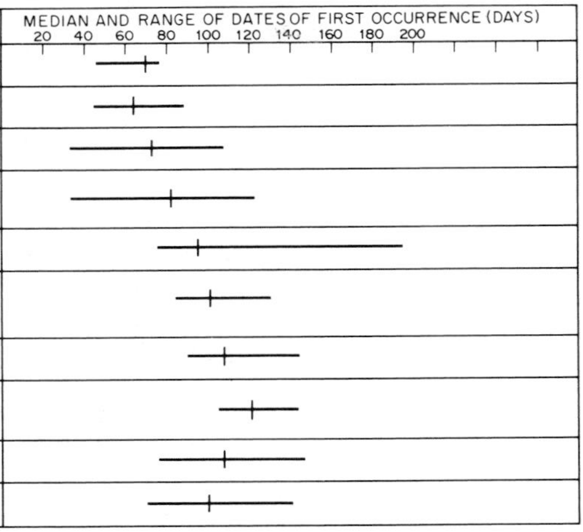

FIG. 22   The development of visually directed reaching for subject in the massive enrichment study.

PREHENSION

The median age for the first appearance of top level reaching was 98 days for the experimental group, an advance of some 45 days over the control group (see Fig. 28). Some kinds of preliminary responses reported for our control group did not occur before the onset of top level reaching.

VISUAL ATTENTION

The course of development of visual attention was also altered dramatically in our experimental group, as illustrated by Figure 23 and Tables 6, 7, and 8. Concurrent with the unexpected delay in the onset of hand regard was a decrease in visual exploratory behavior for the first portion of the test period. On the other hand, once the group began to engage in prehensory contacts with the stabile and the figured bumpers, visual attention increased sharply.

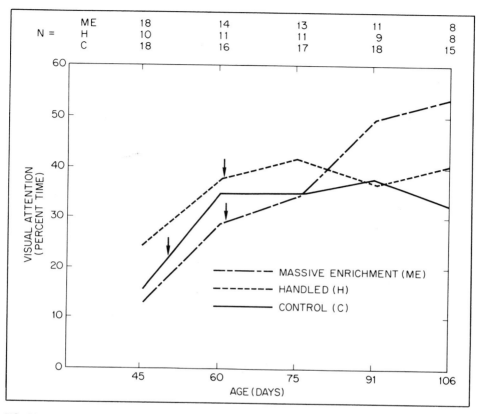

FIG. 23 Comparison of visual attention among control subjects, handled subjects, and those given handling followed by massive enrichment.

DISCUSSION

Clearly, the results of this study demonstrate the plasticity of several visual-motor developments. That the onset of hand regard is in part a function of environmental factors is not novel. Hand regard is a behavior for day 84 on the Gesell scale. Our control infants, with virtually nothing else to look at, discovered their hands before 50 days of age. Piaget (1952) noted that the onset of this behavior varied by as much as 30 days among his own children as a function of differing environmental circumstances. Therefore, the fact that infants provided with enriched surroundings were late in discovering their hands as compared with controls was not totally unexpected.

We were surprised that the group exhibited less visual attention during the first 5 weeks in the enriched visible surroundings. In fact, not only did they tend to ignore the stabile and bumpers, but it is our impression that they engaged in much more

TABLE 6   SUMMARY OF VISUAL ATTENTION DATA

Group and Period Observed	$N_{subjects}$[a]	N_{scores}[a]	Mean Percentage of Time Attending
37–112 days			
Control	45	113	32.1
Handled	11	102	36.8
Massive enrichment	13	118	32.8
Modified enrichment	14	146	40.1
Total	83	479	
37–75 days			
Control	34	59	29.9
Handled	10	58	34.2
Massive enrichment	13	68	26.3
Modified enrichment	14	78	36.7
Total	71	263	
76–112 days			
Control	16	43	33.5
Handled	8	37	41.4
Massive enrichment	9	43	46.9
Modified enrichment	13	70	42.5
Total	46	193	

Source: White (1967). © 1967 University of Minnesota.
[a] Number of subjects and observations varies because subjects, though overlapping, were not identical for the three periods.

crying than did the control group during the same period. Starting at about 72 days of age this group began to engage in a great deal of stabile play. As we had suspected, the rattles were repeatedly swiped at, thereby producing far more monitored hand and arm movements than would normally have occurred. Subsequently, in less than 1 month, the integration of the grasp with approach movements had been completed. Control infants had required almost 3 months for this transition.

Earlier we had noted that the course of development of visual exploratory behavior seemed to reflect the availability of interesting things to look at. We had seen that in control and handled groups the slope of the curve of visual attention increased sharply when the hands were discovered and then decreased during the next 6 weeks. In this experimental group it appears that for a month, starting at day 37, the enrichment was actually ineffective and perhaps even unpleasant. However, once positive responses to the surroundings began to occur, visual attention increased sharply, in striking contrast with the previous groups; the dip seen at 3½ months in both previous groups was absent.

TABLE 7   SUMMARIES OF ANALYSES OF VARIANCE PER-
FORMED ON VISUAL ATTENTION DATA

Treatment Groups in Analysis [a] and Period Observed	Source	ss	df	ms	F	p
37–112 days old						
C, H, ME, Mod E	Between	4696	3	1565	3.95	<.01
	Within [b]	188259	475	396		
	Total	192955	478			
C, H, ME	Between	987	2	494	1.10	NS
	Within [b]	148084	331	447		
	Total	149071	333			
37–75 days old						
C, H, ME, Mod E	Between	4550	3	1517	4.56	<.01
	Within [b]	86137	259	333		
	Total	90687	262			
C, H, Mod E	Between	1615	2	808	2.43	NS
	Within [b]	63714	192	332		
	Total	65329	194			
76–112 days old						
C, H, ME, Mod E	Between	3560	3	1187	2.87	<.05
	Within [b]	78011	189	413		
	Total	81571	192			

Source: White (1967). © 1967 University of Minnesota.

[a] C = Control Group; H = Handled Group; ME = Massive Enrichment Group; Mod E = Modified Enrichment Group.

[b] In nested analysis of variance -designs, between- and within-subject mean squares may be pooled if they do not differ significantly (Winer 1962). In the data of this study, such was the case. Since neither between- nor within-subject variability was of interest, the variances were pooled to test for treatment differences.

THIRD MODIFICATION OF REARING CONDITIONS— THE MODIFIED ENRICHMENT STUDY

Until day 37, procedures for the third study were the same as in the second study, but instead of enrichment by prone placement, the stabile, and printed sheets and bumpers, there was only one modification from days 37 to 68 (White 1967). Two pacifiers were mounted on the crib rails, and were made to stand out visually by appending to them a red and white pattern against a flat white background (Fig. 24). The objects were 6 to 7 inches away from the corneal surfaces of the infant's eyes. They were

TABLE 8   SIGNIFICANCE OF DIFFERENCES BETWEEN MEAN VISUAL ATTENTION SCORES FOR EXPERIMENTAL AND CONTROL GROUPS OBSERVED AT AGE 37–75 DAYS AND/OR 76–112 DAYS

Group Means Compared [a]	t	df	p [b]
37–112 Days Old			
C (32.1) vs. H (36.8)	1.72	213	<.05
C (32.1) vs. ME (32.8)			NS
C (32.1) vs. Mod E (40.1)	3.10	257	<.005
H (36.8) vs. ME (32.8)			NS
H (36.8) vs. Mod E (40.1)			NS
ME (32.8) vs. Mod E (40.1)	2.96	262	<.005
Mod E (40.1) vs. C + H + ME (33.8)	3.50	477	<.0005
37–75 Days Old			
C (29.9) vs. H (34.2)			NS [c]
C (29.9) vs. ME (26.3)			NS
C (29.9) vs. Mod E (40.1)	3.21	135	<.005
H (34.2) vs. ME (26.3)	2.42	124	<.01
H (34.2) vs. Mod E (40.1)	1.87	134	<.05
ME (26.3) vs. Mod E (40.1)	4.56	144	<.0005
ME (26.3) vs. C + H + Mod E (33.9)	2.97	262	<.01
76–112 Days Old			
C (33.5) vs. H (41.4)	1.73	78	<.05
C (33.5) vs. ME (46.9)	3.06	84	<.005
C (33.5) vs. Mod E (42.5)	2.29	111	<.025
H (41.4) vs. ME (46.9)			NS
H (41.4) vs. Mod E (42.5)			NS
ME (46.9) vs. Mod E (42.5)			NS

Source: White (1967). © 1967 University of Minnesota.

[a] C = Control Group; H = Handled Group; ME = Massive Enrichment Group; Mod E = Modified Enrichment Group.

[b] Because six significance figures are being calculated in each group, a conservative position would increase the required level of significance to $10/K(K-1)$, where K = Number of Groups. In this case, K = 4, and the more stringent level required would be .0083 (Ferguson 1959, p. 238).

[c] In a previous report (White and Castle 1964), we indicated that this increase in visual attention was statistically significant. In fact, the analysis used was somewhat inappropriate. In addition, we have added data from one new subject. Subsequent analyses (see White 1967, Tables 3 and 4) indicate a strong trend that fails to reach significance at the .05 level.

positioned so as to elicit maximum attention from 6 to 10 week-old infants, whose eyes normally accommodate at about 8 to 10 inches. It was assumed that the pacifiers might have the effect of orienting the infant toward the discovery of his own hands. It was further assumed that these objects might

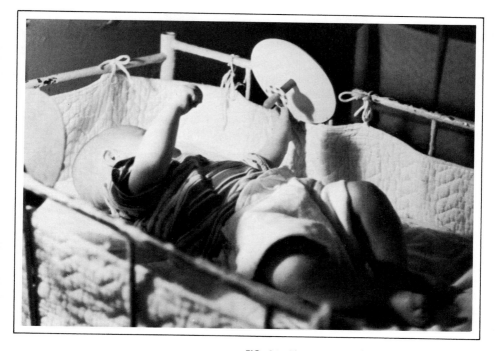

FIG. 24   The modified enrichment condition.

provide appropriate anchor points in space intermediate between the locus of spontaneous fixation and the ordinary path of motion of the hand extended in the tonic neck reflex posture.

At 68 days, the infant was placed in a crib with a stabile similar to the one used in the previous study until he was 124 days of age. We hypothesized that these infants would be more consistently precocious in the attainment of visually directed reaching. We also expected consistently higher visual attention from this group.

RESULTS

HAND REGARD AND SWIPING

In the control group the onset of sustained hand regard occurred at day 49, and infants in the handling study were behind (day 60). Infants in the second study were even later in this respect (day 61), supporting the idea that the discovery of the hand is, in part, a function of the availability of interesting visible objects. The modified enrichment of this study seemed more appropriate for the infant during the second month of life; infants exhibited sustained hand regard at day 44 (see Fig. 28). It should be noted that control infants reared in bland surroundings are about as advanced in hand regard at this age. The onset of swiping responses followed the same general pattern with infants in the third study exhibiting this behavior earlier than all other groups (day 58; see Fig. 25).

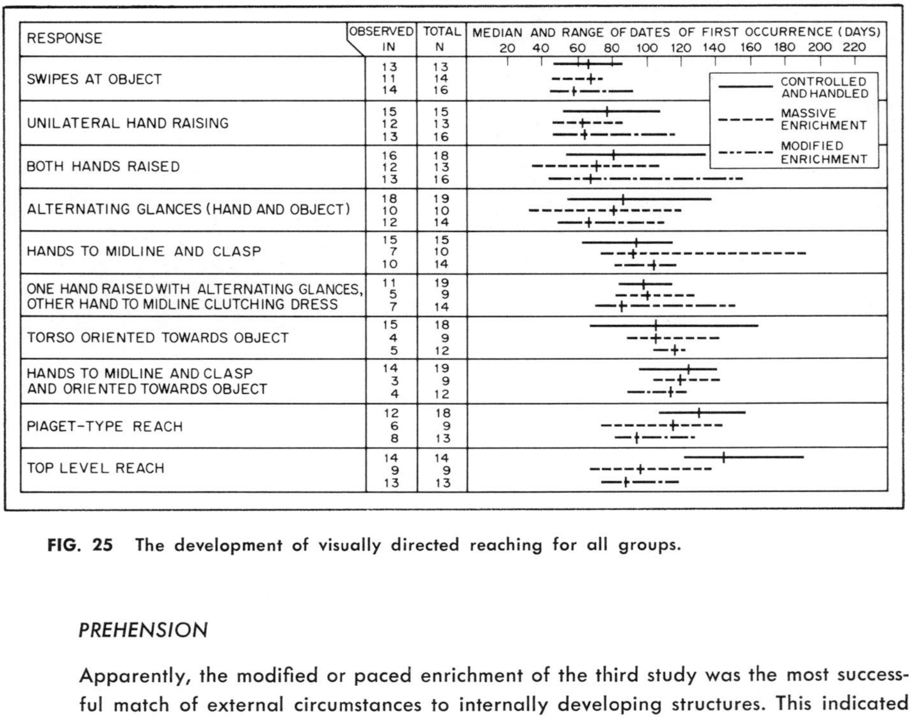

RESPONSE	OBSERVED IN	TOTAL N	MEDIAN AND RANGE OF DATES OF FIRST OCCURRENCE (DAYS)
SWIPES AT OBJECT	13 11 14	13 14 16	
UNILATERAL HAND RAISING	15 12 13	15 13 16	
BOTH HANDS RAISED	16 12 13	18 13 16	
ALTERNATING GLANCES (HAND AND OBJECT)	18 10 12	19 10 14	
HANDS TO MIDLINE AND CLASP	15 7 10	15 10 14	
ONE HAND RAISED WITH ALTERNATING GLANCES, OTHER HAND TO MIDLINE CLUTCHING DRESS	11 5 7	19 9 14	
TORSO ORIENTED TOWARDS OBJECT	15 4 5	18 9 12	
HANDS TO MIDLINE AND CLASP AND ORIENTED TOWARDS OBJECT	14 3 4	19 9 12	
PIAGET-TYPE REACH	12 6 8	18 9 13	
TOP LEVEL REACH	14 9 13	14 9 13	

Legend: CONTROLLED AND HANDLED; MASSIVE ENRICHMENT; MODIFIED ENRICHMENT

FIG. 25 The development of visually directed reaching for all groups.

PREHENSION

Apparently, the modified or paced enrichment of the third study was the most successful match of external circumstances to internally developing structures. This indicated the acquisition of top level reaching at less than three months of age (day 89), significantly earlier than controls, p < .001; Mann-Whitney U Test.

VISUAL ATTENTION

Figure 26 shows visual attention data for the subjects of the 4 groups. The depression of visual interest shown by the infants in the second study from day 37 to 74 has been eliminated, and the modified enrichment group consistently is more attentive throughout the test period (see Tables 6, 7, and 8). Curiously, although the third group was more consistently attentive than the others, the reduction of such behavior

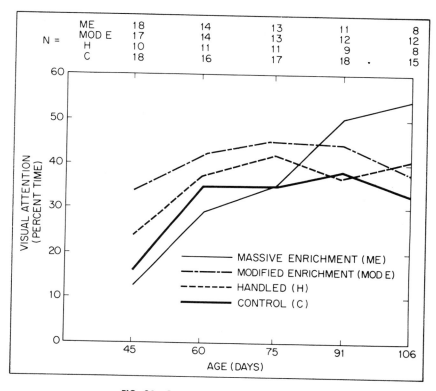

N =	ME	18	14	13	11	8
	MOD E	17	14	13	12	12
	H	10	11	11	9	8
	C	18	16	17	18	15

FIG. 26 Comparison of visual attention among all groups.

at 3½ months appeared as it had in the control and the first groups. It would appear that some uncontrolled variable is interacting with our various attempts at modifying the function.

FOURTH MODIFICATION OF REARING CONDITIONS—
THE MITT STUDY

The three major clusters of experience that seemed appropriate for manipulation during the first three months of life are hand regard, nonspecific visual attention while supine, and visual attention while prone and with head elevated. The purposes of this latest study were to induce earlier acquisition of flexible accommodation and whatever perceptual mechanisms underlie the blink response to approaching visible targets.

The following alterations of rearing conditions were instituted from 21 to 105 days of age. Red and white striped golfer's mitts were worn by experimental subjects (Fig. 27). Their plain white sheets and bumpers were replaced with others featuring various colors and forms. Finally, experimental subjects were placed in the prone position for fifteen minutes after the 6 A.M., 10 A.M., and 2 P.M. feedings. These procedures were designed to hasten the visual discovery of the hands and to provide a more easily perceivable, informative, and interesting visible surround. Whether passive visual scanning or scanning while moving head, torso, and hands is more effective in early development is an open question. We hoped to address the more primitive general question of the plasticity of the behaviors in question by increasing both kinds of learning opportunities.

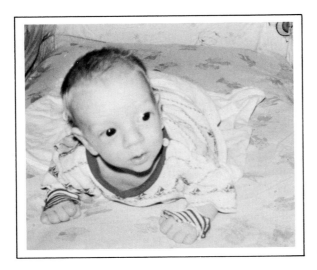

FIG. 27 The exposure conditions for the mitt study.

RESULTS

HAND REGARD

The onset of sustained hand regard was markedly enhanced (Fig. 28).

VISUAL ATTENTION

The total amount of visual attention was unchanged, but the disposition of attention while alert was altered considerably (Figs. 29 and 30). Hand regard occurred in the experimental group as a common activity during most of the second month of life whereas virtually none was seen in the new control group.

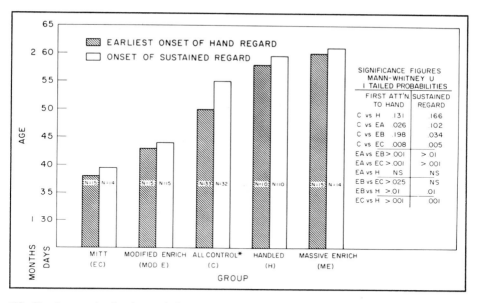

FIG. 28 Comparative hand regard data: median date of onset of brief glances and sustained regard. *Old and new control combined.

VISUAL ACCOMMODATION

No significant change occurred in the development of visual accommodative ability (Table 9). A slight trend may be present since group performance for experimental infants was slightly behind at the outset of the study and slightly ahead by the end.

TABLE 9   THE DEVELOPMENT OF VISUAL ACCOMMODATION
COMPARISON OF CONTROL VS. EXPERIMENTAL
GROUPS

Age (days)		Subjects Control	Experimental	Significance Levels (Mann-Whitney U test)
18–31	N_s	15	9	
	Median slope values	±.40	±.55	N.S.
32–80	N_s	16	26	
	Median slope values	±.19	±.28	N.S.
81–105	N_s	9	12	
	Median slope values	±.10	±.28	N.S.

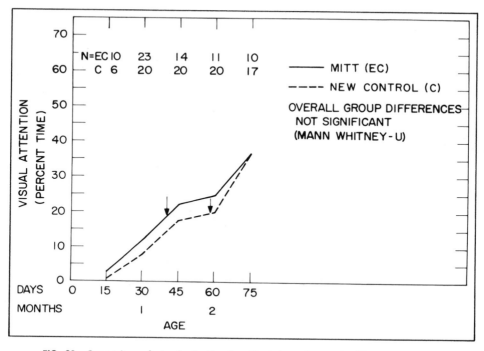

FIG. 29 Comparison of visual attention in mitt study and control subjects.

THE BLINK RESPONSE

Table 10 and Figures 31, 32, and 33 present comparative data on the development of the blink response in the two groups. There is no indication that this process has been significantly affected by the experimental conditions.

EXPERIENCE AND THE DEVELOPMENT OF SENSORIMOTOR INTELLIGENCE DURING THE FIRST SIX MONTHS OF LIFE

A post hoc analysis was performed of the effects of the modified enrichment experiences (see p. 99) on the development of sensorimotor intelligence during the first six months (Piaget 1952). We were primarily interested in whether a custom-built set of rearing conditions would produce accelerated growth of pre-intellectual structures (schemas) com-

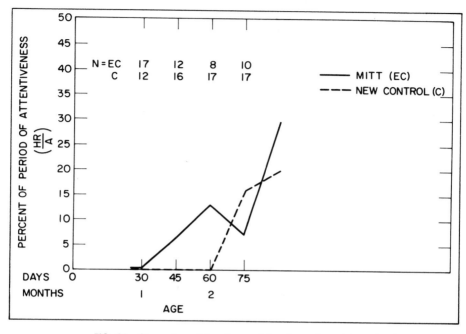

FIG. 30 Comparison of hand regard in mitt study and control subjects.

parable to the enhancements induced in visual-motor processes. Sixteen babies were reared under conditions designed to increase the occurrence of certain forms of motility in sensorily-enriched surrounds. The experimental exposure lasted from day 6 through day 124. In particular, our analysis focused on the coordination and proliferation of schemas. We hypothesized that:

Increased looking at and palpating of nearby objects (induced via enrichment procedures) would result in acceleration of the coordination process.

RESULTS

Is the developmental sequence influenced by rearing conditions? Table 11 contains responses to the object-in-hand test shown by the experimental group. Table 12 indicates that the groups differ significantly.

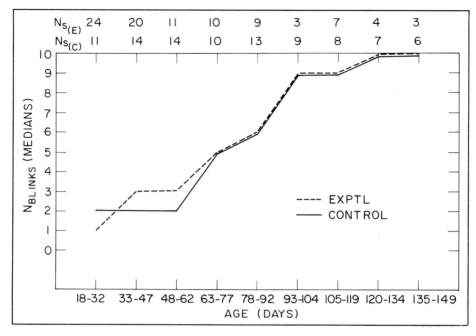

FIG. 31 Blink data—frequency of responses over ten trials—experimental vs. control groups.

FIG. 32 Blink data—latency of responses—experimental vs. control groups.

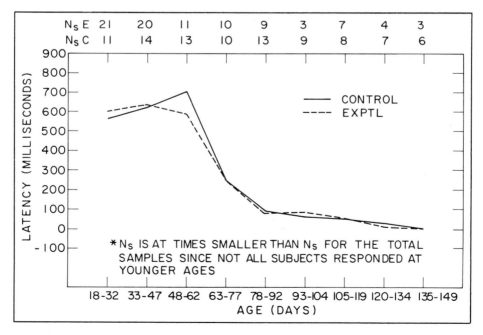

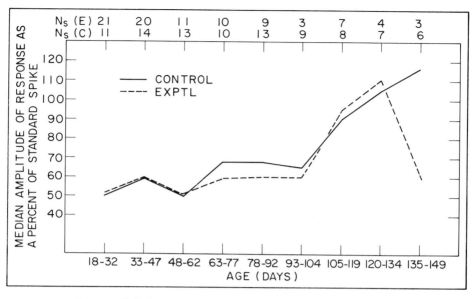

FIG. 33 Blink data—amplitude of response—experimental vs. control groups.

Is the rate of coordination of schemas influenced by rearing conditions? Table 13 shows comparative data for the experimental and control groups. The schemas listed are not necessarily the only ones involved in the behaviors seen.[3]

DISCUSSION

It is clear that the coordination of schemas as described in this analysis had been accelerated for the experimental group. With respect to prehension, the median dates of onset for stages 4 and 5 were 95 to 89 days respectively, compared to 130 and 147 days for the control group. These shifts are highly significant ($p < .001$—Mann-Whitney U test, Siegel 1956).

The prediction of plasticity of development was amply confirmed. The results of

---

[3] Piaget doesn't give precise guidelines for assigning schemas to behavior. I have tried to be conservative in assigning schemas to the behavior patterns in question. There seem to be at least five schemas involved: (1) the grasp schema-retention of the object; (2) the visual schema-glance, or prolonged viewing of the object; (3) the sucking schema—the object is brought to the mouth for attempts at sucking; (4) the tactual schema—the other hand joins with the hand holding the object either to feel it or take it away; and (5) the "other" arm movement schema—the other hand is raised. This last schema reflects the ambiguities in assigning schemas to complicated behavior patterns. Since all behaviors require a schema in Piaget's system, and since hand-raising occurs rather often, I have postulated a schema for it. Actually, hand-raising is a part of another schema, bilateral hand-raising, which is a behavior pattern often seen between 7 and 11 weeks of age in our control group.

TABLE 10 THE DEVELOPMENT OF THE BLINK (PALPEBRAL) RESPONSE TO AN APPROACHING VISIBLE TARGET—COMPARISON OF EXPERIMENTAL VS. CONTROL GROUPS

Age (days):	18–32 E	18–32 C	33–47 E	33–47 C	48–62 E	48–62 C	63–77 E	63–77 C	78–92 E	78–92 C	93–104 E	93–104 C	105–119 E	105–119 C	120–134 E	120–134 C	135–149 E	135–149 C
Target Drop — FREQUENCY																		
2″ N_g	24	11	20	14	11	14	10	10	9	13	3	9	7	8	4	7	3	6
Med	1	1	2	¾	2	½	4	3	4	3	3	6	7	5	7	8	5	9½
Range	0–4	0–4	0–5	0–4	0–3	0–7	0–6	0–8	1–10	0–4	1–5	3–9	5–9	1–10	2–10	3–10	4–10	5–10
7″ N_g	24	11	20	14	11	14	10	10	9	13	3	9	7	8	4	7	3	6
Med	1	3	3	2	2	2	5	8	4	7	10	9	9	10	10	10	10	10
Range	0–6	0–6	0–8	0–10	1–7	0–10	0–9	1–9	1–10	5–10	9–10	8–10	5–10	5–10	4–10	9–10	9–10	9–10
12″ N_g	24	11	20	14	11	14	10	10	9	13	3	9	7	8	4	7	3	6
Med	2	4	4	3	7	5	8	8	9	8	10	10	10	10	10	10	10	10
Range	0–8	1–6	2–10	0–10	2–9	0–10	1–10	3–10	5–10	5–10	4–10	9–10	7–10	3–10	4–10	7–10	8–10	9–10
Overall Median Score Across 2–7–12″	1	2	3	2	3	2	5	5	6	6	9	9	9	9	10	10	10	10
LATENCY																		
2″ N_g	15	6	17	8	9	7	8	8	9	10	3	9	8	8	4	7	3	6
Med	430	500	430	400	500	475	562	425	150	203	180	120	100	73	130	80	70	55
Range	310–1010	340–600	−50–1000	−88–780	300–1060	−120–760	110–918	160–1060	60–650	90–835	0–400	60–400	60–140	40–530	10–570	40–360	40–420	−5–140
7″ N_g	17	7	18	13	11	12	9	10	9	13	3	9	7	8	4	7	3	6
Med	640	460	542	650	460	810	250	200	40	80	100	40	20	25	0	0	0	10
Range	0–1020	360–1060	−120–1040	100–1100	30–920	90–1140	60–1000	60–800	−60–160	0–255	60–400	−5–120	−30–170	−95–200	−80–140	−30–40	−10–20	−80–30

12" N_s	19	11	20	13	11	13	10	10	9	13	3	9	7	8	4	7	3	6
Med	440	650	775	600	800	350	75	35	50	40	40	40	0	5	−30	−20	−20	−15
Range	−260−1200	20−1200	140−1130	0−960	100−1030	0−1050	−20−1200	0−320	−60−400	−50−800	20−80	−30−80	−20−100	−720−100	−60−160	−60−60	−50−0	−125−0
Overall Median Score Across 2−7−12"	540	560	640	570	500	473	250	180	87	85	80	60	50	55	5	30	0	0
AMPLITUDE 2" N_s	15	6	17	8	9	7	8	8	9	10	3	9	7	8	4	7	3	6
Med(%)	45	66	47	66.5	40	47	69	40	50	51	53	57	80	70	85	70	53	116
Range(%)	20−125	30−107	27−147	26−140	27−92	30−120	31−100	25−100	30−113	32−93	50−67	40−67	40−210	25−174	50−120	67−43	40−60	53−144
7" N_s	17	7	18	13	11	12	9	10	9	13	3	9	7	8	4	7	3	6
Med(%)	67	50	79	52	53	53	60	61	67	73	60	87	93	100	95	147	67	114
Range(%)	30−160	30−136	33−200	27−130	26−150	32.5−100	27−160	25−147	40−168	36−140	40−140	40−160	50−160	35−175	25−370	80−214	40−90	67−208
12" N_s	19	11	20	13	11	13	10	10	9	13	3	9	7	8	4	7	3	6
Med(%)	53	56	73	47	67	70	57	80	80	93	70	120	100	106	105	113	90	113
Range(%)	30−220	25−113	26−131	30−107	40−200	27−150	33−107	30−275	40−174	40−140	40−107	53−74	80−153	35−179	80−160	58−166	53−113	98−208
Overall Median Score Across 2−7−12"	60	60	60	53	53	57	60	67	60	73	60	65	95	90	110	105	60	116

Source: White (1969a). Copyright 1969 by Oxford University Press.

TABLE 11 THE SEQUENCE EXHIBITED BY EXPERIMENTAL SUBJECTS

Age (months)	N [a]	Test: Response	Object-In-Hand Subjects Exhibiting N	Response %	N	Prehension Response
1½–2	16	1. Retains only	16	100.0		
		2. Views	10	62.6		
		3. Brought to mouth	6	37.5		
2–2½	16	1. Retains only	15	93.9		
		2. Views	10	62.6		
		3. Views other hand raised	5	31.3		
		4. Views other hand	4	25.0		
		5. Brought to mouth	4	25.0		
2½–3	14	1. Views	13	93.0	13	True reaching (median—89 days)
		2. Retains only	7	50.0		
		3. Views other hand	6	42.8		
		4. Monitored mutual play	5	35.7		
		5. Views other hand	4	28.6		
3–3½	12	1. Views	10	83.6	8	4th stage reaching (median—95 days)
		2. Retains only	7	58.3		
		3. Views other hand	6	50.0		
		4. Monitored mutual play	4	33.3		
		5. Views other hand	3	25.0		
3½–4	12	1. Views	10	83.6		
		2. Monitored mutual play	7	58.3		
		3. Views other hand	4	33.3		
		4. Monitored mutual play then to mouth	3	25.0		
		5. Views then to mouth	1	8.3		
		6. Retains only	1	8.3		
4–4½	11	1. Views	9	82.8		
		2. Monitored mutual play	9	82.8		
		3. Views other hand	4	36.4		
4½–5	9	1. Monitored mutual play	8	88.9		
		2. Views	7	77.8		
		3. Views then to mouth	3	33.3		
		4. Views other hand	3	33.3		
		5. Monitored mutual play then to mouth	2	22.2		
		6. Brought to mouth	0	00.0		

Source: White (1969a). Copyright 1969 by Oxford University Press.
Note: Total N = 90. Total trials = 380.
[a] Average number of tests/subject was 1.90. Average number of responses/trial was 1.13, increasing steadily with age.

TABLE 12   SIGNIFICANCE LEVELS FOR DIFFERENCES BETWEEN
CONTROL AND EXPERIMENTAL SUBJECTS—OBJECT-
IN-HAND TEST

Response	% Subjects Exhibiting Response [a]		t	df	Significance Level (1-tailed test)
	Controls	Experimentals			
Retains only	24.0	8.3	1.34	35	N.S.
Views	13.0	62.6	3.56	37	>.001
Views with other hand raised	7.4	31.3	1.90	41	N.S.
Brought to mouth	37.5	0.0	3.10	23	>.005
Views—other hand	20.0	42.8	1.47	27	N.S.
Monitored mutual play	35.7	64.3	2.79	27	>.005
Monitored mutual play then to mouth	12.0	25.0	0.93	35	N.S.
Views then to mouth	28.0	8.3	1.64	35	N.S.

Source: White (1969a). Copyright 1969 by Oxford University Press.

[a] In this analysis the following procedure was followed:
1. Identify responses that occurred in at least 20% of either group.
2. Determine the number of age periods when each response occurred in at least 20% of either group.
3. Calculate the probability of any single comparison between groups for any two week interval for an overall significance level of .05 according to the following formula:

$$p = (1 - a_i)^n$$

where n = number of 2 weeks periods, and where response occurred in at least 20% of either group.
4. Test most extreme group differences against adjusted significance levels.

N	1	2	3	4	5	6	7
a_i	.050	.025	.017	.012	.010	.008	.007

both the object-in-hand and the prehension tests indicate important functional relationships between rearing conditions and the developmental process in question.
Further, the degree of acceleration involved in the experimental group is more than
nominal even though the experimental modifications of rearing conditions were little
more than first attempts. Of course, at this time no claim can be made for precise
understanding of the role of experience; however, some discussion of the design of
the experimental rearing conditions is in order at this point.

During the first six months of life children are not usually able to locomote; in
fact, they have limited abilities in most all developmental areas. In addition, their
experiential histories are very brief. These factors combined suggest that an analysis

TABLE 13 DISTRIBUTION OF SCHEMAS AS A FUNCTION OF AGE FOR CONTROL AND EXPERIMENTAL GROUPS— OBJECT-IN-HAND TEST

Age (months)	CONTROL				EXPERIMENTAL			
	Response [a]	Schemas Involved [b]	% Showing	Weighted Score	Response	Schemas Involved	% Showing	Weighted Score
1½–2	Retains only	1	95.8	95.8	Retains only	1	100.0	100.0
	Brought to mouth	2	21.7	43.4	Views	2	62.6	125.2
					Brought to mouth	2	37.5	75.0
Group score:				139.2				300.2
2–2½	Retains only	1	85.2	85.2	Retains only	1	93.9	93.9
					Views	2	62.6	125.2
					Views other hand raised	3	31.3	93.9
					Views other hand	2	25.0	50.0
					Brought to mouth	2	25.0	50.0
Group score:				85.2				413.0
2½–3	Retains only	1	84.1	84.1	Views	2	93.0	186.0
	Views	2	72.1	144.2	Retains only	1	50.0	50.0
					Views other hand	2	42.8	85.6
					Monitored mutual play	3	35.7	107.1
					Views—other hand raised	3	28.6	85.8
Group score:				228.3				514.5
3–3½	Views	2	89.0	178.0	Views	2	83.6	167.3
	Retains only	1	59.3	59.3	Retains only	1	58.3	58.3
	Monitored mutual play	3	25.9	77.7	Views other hand raised	3	50.0	150.0
	Brought to mouth	2	22.2	44.4	Monitored mutual play	3	33.3	99.9
					Views other hand	2	25.0	50.0
Group score:				359.4				535.4

Age group 3½–4

Response				Response			
Views	2	80.0		Views	2	83.6	167.2
Monitored mutual play	3	52.0		Monitored mutual play	3	58.3	174.9
Views then to mouth	3	28.0		Views other hand raised	3	33.3	99.9
Retains only	1	24.0		Monitored mutual play	4	25.0	100.0
Views other hand raised	3	24.0					
		72.0					
Group score:		544.0		Group score:			542.0

Age group 4–4½

Response				Response			
Views	2	81.0		Views	2	82.8	165.6
Monitored mutual play	3	71.5		Monitored mutual play	3	82.8	248.4
Views other hand raised	3	33.3		Views other hand raised	3	36.4	109.2
Group score:		476.5		Group score:			523.2

Age group 4½–5

Response				Response			
Views	2	75.0		Monitored mutual play	3	88.9	266.7
Monitored mutual play	3	56.3		Views	2	77.8	155.6
Brought to mouth	2	37.5		Views then to mouth	3	33.3	99.9
Views then to mouth	3	37.5		Views other hand raised	3	33.3	99.9
				Monitored mutual play then to mouth	4	22.2	88.8
Group score:		506.4		Group score:			710.9

Source: White (1969a). Copyright 1969 by Oxford University Press.

Note: Group differences are significant beyond .02 level—Randomization test (Siegel, 1956).

a Only responses occurring in at least 20% of the subjects are included.

b Schemas were assigned as follows:

Response	Schemas Involved	Total Schemas
1. Retains only	Grasp	1
2. Brought to mouth	Grasp; Sucking	2
3. Views	Grasp; Vision	2
4. Views—other hand	Grasp; Vision	2
5. Views—other hand raised	Grasp; Vision; "Other Arm"; Movement	3
6. Views then to mouth	Grasp; Vision; Sucking	3
7. Monitored mutal play	Grasp; Vision; Tactual	3
8. Monitored mutual play then to mouth	Grasp; Vision; Tactual; Sucking	4

of the opportunities for learning is more feasible for this period than for subsequent ones. Piaget has provided some clues by describing the developing sensorimotor structures. Only lengthy longitudinal observations can complete the picture, however. These, we have done for one population. We have observed several hundred physically normal, hospital reared infants for three continuous hours each week from birth to six months (White et al., 1964; White and Castle 1964).

The favorite activities of these children when awake and not distressed or drowsy are visual exploration, especially of their own hands, tactual exploration, and combined visual and tactual exploration, again usually of their own hands. From about the fourteenth week on, if given the opportunity, they will usually view areas several yards away. However, when placed in the prone position prior to that time, their visual and tactual interest seems to be restricted primarily to the 24 inches or so around them. On the basis of unsystematic observations, it would appear that home reared babies do not differ radically in these respects. The major visual-motor activities of this time of life primarily consist of the internal ocular adjustments of accommodation and position including convergence and pursuit; rotations of the head; movements of the arm, hand, and fingers within the visual field; head rearing (in the prone position); and, from about the fifth month on, turning of the torso from side to side, and occasionally completely over.

Our modified enrichment group was given extra handling during the first 36 days of life when visual-motor activities do not occupy much of the infant's day (White and Held 1966; White 1967). During the second month an attempt was made to optimize learning conditions for the acquisition of visual control over the hand which seems to be a major if not *the* major sensorimotor acquisition of the first half year of life. Visually-monitored batting and tactual exploration of nearby objects was induced (White and Held 1966; White 1967). During the third month, similar activities plus heightened visual scanning was induced by the presence of new viewable and palpable objects as well as routine prone placement of the subjects (White and Held 1966; White 1969a).

Obviously, we have dealt with molar experiences rather than isolated independent variables. The scientific task that awaits is the sorting of what is and what is not relevant within the gross experimental treatment. It is here that refined theory is sooner or later necessary; however, I do not believe that one should proceed hastily toward extended theoretical analyses. Rather, I would advocate modest theoretical distinctions followed by empirical test leading to new theoretical deviations slightly more specific, followed by test, etc. (see Chapter 4). Of obvious importance for developmental psychology is the demonstration of the functional relevance of experience to the developments in question. Although this study requires replication and is only an early attempt in a complicated area of investigation, it appears that major effects on the rate of development may be induced with ease using innocuous alterations in rearing conditions. Let me point out, however, that the design of enrichment conditions in this study or "the match" as Hunt would put it, presupposes dependable knowledge about infant capacities and preferences. This information is expensive to obtain, coming as it does from hundreds of hours of naturalistic observations and the results of standardized test sessions.

6

MAJOR ISSUES
IN
CURRENT RESEARCH

I MUST ADMIT AT THIS POINT to a very strong bias. Unless theoretical or explanatory statements about experience and human infant development have strong empirical backing, preferably from experimental data from studies of *human* infants, I tend not to pay them much attention. The question of how to rear the better baby is so glamorous, so attractive to society, and so fraught with emotionalism that it invites precipitous judgments and ungrounded speculations. The fact is that direct, experimentally-validated evidence on the role of experience in human development is almost non-existent. What does one do in such a situation? My recommendation is that we should proceed with caution, maintaining a careful coordination between the elaboration of theory and the growth of relevant data.

SOME IMPLICATIONS AND POSSIBLE SEQUELAE OF LONGITUDINAL-EXPERIMENTAL WORK ON THE ROLE OF EXPERIENCE IN INFANT DEVELOPMENT

The series of enrichment studies described in the proceeding chapter is relatively unique. Those studies, along with the handful cited in Chapter 3, almost exhaust the category, "Experimental studies of the role of experience in the development of human infants." There are several reasons for such longitudinal-experimental research with human infants not usually being done. First of all, most of us have ambivalent feelings about experimentation with humans. The typical 15-minute experiment on motor-reaction time using adult human subjects rarely gives us moral rumblings, but inducing even modest, short-term traumas is problematical, and procedures with children which are not totally benign are virtually forbidden. Little wonder then that experiments where control is exerted over large portions of an infant's daily experience may generate some negative feelings. The fact that all infants are being subjected to some pattern of experience and that out of lack of knowledge that pattern at times may not be good for them is often overlooked. After all, no one has identified the one "natural" or the correct way to rear infants. And yet, if it is through the cumulative effects of countless small encounters with the world that the infant learns, then surely the legitimate scientific route for understanding those developments must involve some form of long-term experimentation.

Our way of coping with this situation has been to systematically enrich the experiences of a population of normal infants who were being reared under bland conditions. Our experimental procedures have always been cleared with the responsible medical personnel prior to use, and no procedure has even been used if doubt existed about its innocuousness.

A second major reason for such studies rarely being done is that the typical doctoral training program doesn't prepare people to do such work. One would hardly expect the student from either a clinical program with its emphasis on diagnostic testing or remedial therapy, or an experimental program with its emphasis on the traditional cross-sectional, highly focused experimental research to inaugurate longitudinal-experimental work. Perhaps the best place to acquire a background for such work would be an institution that concerns itself with the effects of early experience on other species. The University of Wisconsin Primate Laboratory under the direction of Harlow, or the Jackson Laboratories at Bar Harbor, or the Delta Primate Laboratory at Tulane, are three possible sites for such training. Most of our programs in human development, however, do not feature research on the role of early experience in human development in the sense that I have described it.

A third probable reason for the scarcity of such studies is that there is usually a larger cost involved. Human infants are precious, they grow slowly compared to mice or even monkeys, they are surrounded and protected by adults, they are complex creatures, and they are, as previously mentioned, usually available only one at a time.

What, then, is the state of knowledge about the role of experience in infant development? The data that exists have convinced me that development during the first 6 months of life is markedly plastic. Of course, we have always known that plasticity existed with respect to poor development.

The extreme point on the negative end of the continuum of development is no development or death. Somewhat closer to the central tendency is the kind of development cited by Spitz (1945) and Dennis and Najarian (1957). Their subjects demonstrated plasticity of early development by virtue of their markedly retarded states during late infancy. One could hold the position that such infants were simply deprived of the minimally necessary ingredients required in order for the genetically determined developmental patterns to unfold. The norms described by Gesell and Amatruda (1941) and Buhler and Hetzer (1935), and those implied in Piaget's work (1952) would then constitute the standard to which all children would develop given minimally adequate care. The fact of individual differences in early development would be attributed to miscellaneous factors such as genetic variation, birth effects, etc. Studies such as ours, however, which show the onset of sustained hand regard (in apparent response to differences in rearing conditions) varying from as early as 35 to as late as 95 days don't fit into such a nativistic scheme of things. This is especially the case when experimental children are consistently much more precocious than the typical home reared child. (See Table 5 and Fig. 28). When the hand regard data are reinforced by controlled precocity in the acquisition of visually-directed reaching, the growth of coordinated sensorimotor schemas, and the increase in visual exploratory behavior, the argument becomes relatively solid. Marked plasticity of sensorimotor and intellectual development during the first 6 months of life is most likely.

But how far have we gone toward understanding the role of experience in infant development? When one considers that within the area of the topics covered in our work we have only investigated five crudely controlled sequences of experiences, and that the order within each sequence could be rearranged in infinite ways, it immediately becomes clear that only the barest beginnings have been executed. One hundred competent developmental psychologists working several decades each would probably not fully unravel the complexities of the interrelationships among the major processes developing simultaneously within infants and the cumulating consequences of the multi-dimensional stimuli which impinge on those infants in new ways thousands of times each day. If all this sounds staggering, then my message may be getting through. In the face of such complexity one sees the inappropriateness of a self-confident air when one is attempting to analyze development with an S-R paradigm (Bijou 1968). Even the valiant efforts of Gewirtz (1969) in attempting a conceptualization of a chain of stimulus-response units are obviously woefully oversimple and doomed to failure.

What is the answer? As important as the problem of early human development is, we still must admit that we have no answer. The experimental approach I have advocated and utilized (see Chapters 4 and 5) is no more than a preliminary, somewhat halting step. At least it is a beginning. To do much better would require a more sophisticated philosophy of science than now exists.

Where do we go from here?

Our research suggests many new directions. We abandoned the investigation of the consequences of extra handling during the first weeks of life after only one attempt, but I am convinced that such experience is admirably suited to the sensory-processing capacity of the child less than six weeks of age. Two other studies of this type have been performed with human infants. In Chapter 3, I cited the work of Ourth and Brown, and Casler. To my knowledge, these three small studies exhaust the list of experimental studies of the effects of handling in early human development.

Our work has suggested that the onset of hand regard and haptic explorations might be optimally induced by combining the procedures of two of our studies. Red and white mitts worn by infants produced earlier visual attention to the hand but no increase in total visual alertness. Handling during the first month followed by regular exposure to suitably marked pacifiers on either side of the infant produced markedly heightened visual attention. Combining handling with palpable visible targets such as the pacifiers and the mitts should be ideal for "feeding" both processes. One should note, however, that gearing early experiences in the direction of hand-eye activity may not be the most advisable procedure when viewed against the total economy of the age period in question.[1]

Providing extra handling, mitts to enlighten the perceptability of the fists, and brightly marked and palable stimuli such as the pacifiers (see Chapter 5) would probably be most conducive to the early onset of sustained hand regard and heightened visual interest. The consequence would be that infants would be viewing their hands regularly at about 5 weeks of age (the norm based on Gesell's sample of home reared infants is 12

---

[1] What I am addressing here is another complication in our fascinating problem. Our enrichment procedures may be suitable for visual-motor and intellectual development, but could conceivably turn out to be less than optimal for social development, for example. The merit of any "curriculum" can only be judged in the light of a complete array of developmental goals. This, of course, has not yet been described for the early months of life. Such an array would inevitably involve the acquisition of visual-motor skills, intellectual sub-structures and their coordination, but also the foundations of attachment behavior and perhaps several others. Until the comprehensive picture is available, we must qualify all statements about the suitability of any set of rearing conditions.

weeks). Further, the visual "heyday" cited by both Gesell and Amatruda (1941) and Piaget (1952) as starting around the beginning of the third month might occur as much as one month earlier. These would be major differences indeed in the brief lives of such infants.

The next stage of an experimental curriculum could be designed to bring the child from the visual discovery of his own hands on to the use of them as primary tools for the early exploration of the proximal environment. The expected age of acquisition of visually-directed reaching is about 5 months. We have already been able to produce reliable visually-directed reaching at 3 months. I suspect the date could ultimately be pushed back to 2½ months. I doubt that we will do much better in the near future because of several factors. First of all, I believe that as long as birth is achieved in the conventional way, the abrupt transition from interuterine to postnatal existence will probably require some recuperative period. Also, there is the large question of the general maturational state of the newborn which apparently is considerably more primitive than what it becomes a few months later. Further, and no doubt related, is the fact of the habitually clenched fists of the infant less than 8 weeks of age, which preclude much prehensory activity. Finally, other prerequisite functions such as visual acuity, accommodation, and convergence are generally inadequately developed prior to 8 to 10 weeks (see Chapter 4).

Were infants reared so that they were routinely reaching for grasping and examining objects from the middle of the third month on, what would come next? According to Piaget (1952), "intellectual" development should proceed to the next stage which would feature the exploration of the grasping and releasing activity with objects, then on to an interest in the paths of motions of objects, etc., up until objects attained independent conceptual existence. How much these and related processes such as the development of conceptions of causality, etc., could be enhanced is a totally open question, but surely it appears that plasticity in the acquisition of visually-directed reaching is of primary importance in the early stages of these processes.

Moving into the area of attachment behavior, the prospects are much less clear. The prerequisite developments and their experiential influences are not as well understood. Bowlby's impressive analysis (1958) of the process points to the social smiling of the third month and the stranger reaction of the eighth month as major links in the developmental chain. It is likely that relationships exist between the emergence of these indicators of social development and early sensorimotor skills. For example, one modality underlying the social smile is vision; another is sound. To the extent that visual and auditory capacities are enhanced, there would probably be cross-over effects on social development. It is quite conceivable that early handling experience may play some role as another precondition of the emergence of the social smile. Beyond this point, we have even less to go on.

OTHER CURRENT ISSUES

The majority of the current American studies deal with a small number of problems. The detection of perceptual capacities, especially those which are innate, is one popular topic. Another is the question of conditionability. An old favorite is the mother-child relation. Recently there has been an increasing interest in temperamental characteristics of individual children and early language. Certainly, the largest effort in recent work has been directed toward the detection of visual perceptual capacities of the 4-day-old infant.[2] In a recent survey of professional effort (LaCrosse et al. in press), we estimate that about 20 per cent of all developmental psychologists studying human infants were studying molecular aspects of vision, and most of them were studying infants less than 1 week old.

There are two kinds of issues in the field of infancy, those generated from work with normal human infants and those transferred from studies with other subjects. By far, the issues that have received the most attention have been of the latter type. The reasons have been alluded to in Chapter 2. Primarily they are two: (1) The exploratory work of science from which one generates indigenous issues is actively discouraged by the prevailing customs in the field, and (2) so little is actually known about the total fabric of the behavior of infants that we are in a poor position to identify specific issues.

Examples of imported issues are: (1) How soon can infants be conditioned? (2) When does the infant exhibit size constancy, depth perception, and a host of other classically-defined perceptual abilities? (3) How does the infant reveal his sexual-aggressive nature? (4) What are his invariant instinctive motor behaviors? These concerns were generated by studies of: (1) dogs, cats, and mice; (2) adult human and other animals; (3) emotionally disturbed adult humans; and (4) birds, fish, and insects.

In contrast, the following concerns are examples of issues which emanate from direct studies of normal infants: How does the infant shift from a

---

[2] As is well known by now, the 4-day-old human infant is challenging the white rat and the college sophomore for the affections of psychologists. The less than 4-day-old infant is often too groggy to study because of the after-effects of birth, and the infant older than 4 days has left the hospital. Furthermore, per-subject cost is low because the infants are available gratis and in groups in hospital maternity wards.

primarily reflexive stereotyped mode of function at birth to the more variegated and increasingly coordinated style of behavior which seems to take over beginning at about three months of age? What are the environmental conditions that encourage the emergence and growth of the capacity for sustained focal attention at two months, the curiosity and euphoria omnipresent in the three and four month old, the freedom from stimulus control which seems to characterize the infant increasingly from three months on, and the intellectual structures or schemas which enable the human infant to outdistance the young of the other species during the first two years of life? What particular stimulus value has an infant for his care-taking adults, and what are the consequences of his way of being treated on his subsequent development? What is the relevance of early vocalizations to the development of language, and what environmental circumstances affect the emergence of such phenomena? How does the infant construct a conceptually independent world of objects with its associated laws of function?

Within a few decades I expect we will have identified many times more the number of issues indigenous to human infancy than we have now. At that time a comparison of the issues and phenomena of human infant behavior with parallel data from other species will provide the foundation for a truly comparative psychology. Such comparative study will unquestionably strengthen the pursuit of knowledge of each of the species involved. In the meantime, we labor under a distinct disadvantage.

What follows is a more extended discussion of a few of the primary issues in early development.

Depth perception

Concepts such as form discrimination and depth perception must be tied to the realities and complexities of infant behavior. Gibson and Walk talk about depth perception in terms of the crawling responses of the eight-month-old child (1960). Fantz reports increased visual orienting to solid rather than to two-dimensional targets after two months of age (1961). More recently, T. Bower has noted cardiac responses to "looming" visual objects in infants less than two months old. We have noted visual accommodative and convergence responses to nearby objects at six weeks, accurate swiping at objects at two months, accurate reaching at three to five months, blinking to an approaching object beginning at two months, and the placing response at about eight months. What shall we call depth perception? My point is that *all* of these data must be considered when studying the development of depth perception. A similar case can be made for form discrimination.

Some primitive capacity for "depth perception" appears to be present at birth. There is a clear relationship between the stimulation produced by the leading edge of a laterally moving object which elicits visual-motor pursuit in the alert newborn (Wolff and White 1965) and the streaming of stimulation to the peripheral areas of the visual field which results from the approach of a visible object. Consider, for example, the stimulation produced by a bull's eye target, such as the red and white disc we use to elicit the blink response, when it falls towards the infant. The set of concentric circles produces a pattern of stimuli radiating peripherally as the target nears the infant. To the extent that the infant's gaze is captured by any of the lateral motion of the pattern, he may be undergoing a visual experience with functional similarity to the situation where he is induced to pursue an object moving across his visual field. Since by exhibiting a crude capacity for visual-motor pursuit the newborn reveals that he is capable of perceiving (in some fashion) a contour moving in the peripheral field, then given certain kinds of conditions wherein depth perception is being tested, he should reveal some signs of "depth perception," such as a heart rate or GSR change. Further, he should manifest such "perceptual ability" when alert and inactive from birth.

The fact that a newborn infant can respond to some element of a visible stimulus complex produced by an approaching object does not mean that what is meant by "depth perception" is innate. What it does suggest, however, and what the previously cited findings suggest is that the term "depth perception" must be defined carefully, especially when it is a bone of contention between nativists and empiricists. Granting some rudimentary innate capacity to detect an aspect of the complex stimulus consequences of an approaching object, does this mean the infant has "depth perception"? Can the neonate discriminate between an approaching object and one that merely grows larger while remaining at a constant distance from him? Can he tell the difference between a three-dimensional object and a drawing of one? Further, it should be remembered that the elementary capacity that exists is only functional under a very restricted range of conditions. The speed, locus of travel, and physical characteristics of the target must all fall within certain narrow limits or the infant will give no evidence of perception.

Superordinate behaviors

Visually directed reaching depends upon the acquisition of several simpler skills such as visual-motor pursuit, sustained fixation, orienting of the head and trunk, the integration of the grasp with the arm approach, and a relatively sophisticated capacity to bring the hand quickly to an infinite number of points in nearby space. Creeping and walking are other examples of superordinate behaviors. We need to know how each prerequisite system develops and the manner in which these systems become subsumed under the superordinate action.

Neonatal visual behavior—active visual search and information processing or passive centralizing reflex?

A rash of reports over the last ten years, triggered in large part by the work of Fantz (1961*a*, 1961*b*, and 1964), has conveyed the impression to some that the newborn, contrary to previously held views, is a remarkably adroit visual creature. Several other investigators, including this writer, believe that this is not the case, but rather that the newborn, and in fact the infant less than six weeks or so of age, is (1) not capable of any but the most primitive visual function and (2) not often engaged in visual inquiry. This disagreement, while not clearly defined, does exist and does underly different postures on the nativism-empiricism controversy. Fantz (1961*b*) represents the more nativistic position and sees the neonatal infant as considerably more able in the visual modality than I do, while both of us regard the neonate as considerably more advanced than did William James.

There is little question now about whether newborns direct their gaze at visible targets. Many studies agree that they do, and no recent findings challenge that view. It is the quality of the activity that is in dispute. Fantz and others of his persuasion argue that the time spent by the newborn gazing at geometric or facial patterns is qualitatively no different from the visual explorations of the three month old or, indeed, the older infant and child. Others, including myself, point to several lines of evidence which indicate that there is a very large difference indeed between the visual behavior of the neonate and the three month old. For one thing, data on focusing ability (visual accommodation) (Haynes, White, and Held 1965) and visual attention (White and Held 1966) reveal that the neonate is (1) rarely alert (see Figs. 8 and 14*a* and *b*) and even with his eyes open is moving in and out of states of sleep or drowsiness, and (2) unable to focus a clear image of targets except very briefly at one very limited distance ($\pm$ an inch or so) from his eyes. For another, the Salapatek data (1966) on line of sight patterns, gathered with an ingenious and reliable photographic technique, indicate that the neonate does not systematically scan an entire target but tends instead to home in on about one feature, for example, one apex of a triangle. Add to this the dramatic achievements in vision at about the end of the second month such as almost adult plasticity of focusing ability, functional adequacy of visual convergence, blinking to approaching visible forms, sustained hand regard, dramatically heightened visual interest, etc., and the case against mature visual function at birth is solid.

What is most likely to be happening at birth is one of many stimulus-bound behaviors, wherein provided that the stimulation is functionally massive, and the conditions (including the infant's state) are optimal, a primitive centralizing reflex may be elicited with fair regularity. Additional support for this view comes from the fact that when visual pursuit is elicited in the newborn, the infant centralizes the target moving in the periphery, but if that target does not subsequently move, the infant's gaze quickly drifts away. In sum, though the newborn is more capable than we thought until the pioneering work of Fantz, he is still a largely inept and nonvisual creature, not only in comparison to a young child, but even in comparison to the three month old.

Learning

One of the more popular areas of research on infant development is learning. There seem to be two major positions prevalent in the field, one espoused by advocates of various conditioning theories, the other by the adherents of a Piagetian orientation. Earlier (see Chapter 2), I briefly discussed what has been variously called the "learning" or "conditioning" or "associationistic" work. At that time, I suggested that while I believed that potentially valuable techniques for future diagnostic and therapeutic work had been developed in these studies, I did not believe they represented the wisest way to investigate how infants learn. I cited the fact that it was only with great skill and elaborate reduction and control of stimulus inputs that modest short-lived learning effects were produced in young infants; that this situation contrasts sharply with the apparently substantial amount of learning which seems to take place routinely in infancy under the uncontrolled, "noisy," and complicated conditions of every day life; and that in any case the necessarily simple experimental paradigms underlying such classical work seemed grossly inappropriate as models for the complicated processes and events we seek to understand.

The Piagetian point of view differs radically from that of the conditioners. Instead of focusing on the pattern of rewards the environment delivers one at a time to an apparently empty organism, the Piagetians present the grand view of development. They talk of schemas, hypothetical mental structures which mediate the transactions of an organism pictured as considerably more than a repository for an atomistically acquired experiential history. They are much more concerned about the particular behaviors the infant comes equipped with and their relation to biological adaptation and ontogenetic development. Unfortunately, next to no empirical work has been done by this group as yet. Still, a large number of my colleagues have more faith in the Piagetian route to understanding how an infant learns than in the pursuits advocated by the conditioners. The Piagetians will have to get much more specific about actual behavior, however, than they have so far.

When I attempted to test some Piagetian ideas about the first months of life (Chapters 4 and 5), I quickly learned that concepts such as assimilation, accommodation, and schema are of little limited direct use when one faces the complexities of actual infant behavior. An enormous amount of work must be done in identifying, sorting, and relating behaviors according to the Piagetian system. In addition, if the conditioners' views are overly simple and handicapped by lack of attention to what motivates an infant, the Piagetian is faced with the problem of defining and working with the concepts of "schema disequilibrium" and "familiarity." These concepts lie at the heart of any experimental attempts by Piagetians to promote early learning. McCall and Kagan (1967) have made one of the few attempts to deal with the problem of quantifying the familiarity dimension, but this is a very complicated question which may require more for its solution than we are currently able to provide.

The transition from innate stereotyped behavior to mature forms

Some twenty years ago, Myrtle McGraw wrote of an initial period of subcortically mediated behavior which gradually disappeared during the first half-year of life as the higher centers matured (1963). During the first few months of life, behavior was stereotyped and mechanical. Thereafter, it became more fluid and variable. Ling, in her study of the development of fixation, described a five-step process which expressed the same general theme (1942). I have seen this kind of qualitative shift in several developing response systems. For example, tactually-induced rooting responses are present at birth. During the first month, response accuracy increases and latency decreases. In general, the infant gradually develops a machine-like stereotyped performance. During the next two months, the behavior drops out and is replaced by what looks like voluntary multi-step searchings with mouth. The development of visual-motor pursuit looks quite similar. Under restricted conditions, rudimentary pursuit is present at birth, but it is difficult to elicit, is discontinuous, and is usually limited in range. (Wolff and White 1965). During the next six weeks, there is an orderly development into a remarkably dependable, smooth performance. At six weeks and for about another month and a half, virtually any infant can be *made* to pursue a moving target (Fig. 34) steadily as long as he is awake. By four to five months, infants usually throw a casual glance at the target and quickly turn away as if to say, "If that's the best you can do, don't waste my time."

This kind of sequence seems to hold for the blink response and visual accommodation and even perhaps for visually-directed reaching. The implications of such developmental sequences are important. Perhaps most basic is that in experimental interventions a recognition of the stage of development of a subject may make it considerably easier to shape and predict behaviors. In addition, it is worth considering whether the conditions for learning are necessarily comparable for different levels of function.

Early perceptual-motor behavior and cognitive development

Our experience indicates that during the first month of life the human infant seems relatively uninterested in his sensory surroundings except for

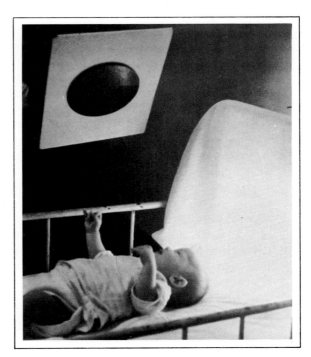

FIG. 34 The visual pursuit target.

scattered intervals of time, rarely exceeding a few minutes in length (Fig. 8). Toward the middle of the second month, however, a marked change sets in. Though unable to move about, the infant begins to exhibit a rapidly increasing interest in his immediate environment. At first this takes the form of head and eye movements predominantly, since his hands are normally not yet open sufficiently for the purpose of tactual exploration. Within the next few weeks, the infant begins to observe his own hand and subsequently spends hundreds of hours gaining visual control over its motions. Simultaneously, tactual explorations become a regular part in the daily routine. It must be a curious sensation after having built up familiarity with the tactual experiences of one's hands individually to experience their coalescence as the hands engage in mutual fingering for the first time. It is this intersection of two previously independent sensorimotor subsystems which Piaget, and von Euxkill before him, have used to provide the theoretical basis for a fundamental cognitive development—the object concept.

In Piaget's system, a target, such as a small toy, has no conceptual existence for the newborn infant. It may serve to evoke innately-organized responses such as grasping and pursuit, but once these actions cease, there is no reason to assume that the toy "exists" in any conceptual way for the neonate. When, however, the infant develops to the point that he makes a prehensory contact with the toy, something qualitatively new appears. That one toy has elicited visual fixation, appropriate arm movements, and tactual contact followed by grasping. Several previously separate action systems intersect at the toy. The toy acquires the beginnings of an independent conceptual existence in so far as it is no longer merely a part of any single action pattern, but now ties several subsystems together. True cognitive representation doesn't develop until many months later in Piaget's system, but prehensory efforts such as reaching do constitute the major early vehicle for this achievement. I don't mean to claim that Piaget's theory is necessarily correct in this respect. But I can't think of a more convincing one at this time.

Our attempts at manipulating prehensory development seem to show that there is significant plasticity in this system as a function of early experience. Some of our experimental subjects are swiping at and reaching for objects much earlier and far more often than they would ordinarily have done (Figs. 22 and 25). To the extent that Piaget's ideas have validity, these very young subjects should be acquiring large amounts of cognitively relevant information. Empirical tests of such ideas would seem in order.

Analytical studies of the role of experience

Our enrichment conditions have usually produced increased motility of several kinds, as well as increased opportunities to view various visible forms and colors. We have induced head and trunk motions by placing infants on their stomachs and also by suspending appropriate objects over their upper bodies. We have evoked repeated, monitored, prehensory movements within custom-designed visual surroundings. These changes in rearing conditions were all initiated and maintained simultaneously in our earlier studies because we needed an answer to the general problem of whether sensorimotor development was significantly affected by experience. More highly focused studies would have been premature and very risky in view of the immaturity of the research effort.

Such multiple independent variable manipulations must be replaced by more analytical studies if we are to attain precision in our understanding. The effects of increased motility versus those of enriched visible circumstances must be isolated. Subsequent analyses of different kinds of movements such as head and trunk versus arm and hand, and rotation versus translation should be investigated. Comparable analyses of the sensory factors also ought to be done.

I have listed several kinds of higher-order issues which seem to demand consideration if we are to gain a greater depth of understanding of early development. I don't think it would be wise at this time for us to abandon completely the parametric studies of isolated functions to concentrate on these larger issues. But I do think these issues may serve an heuristic purpose as indicators of which directions to pursue. For the next twenty years or so, I would prefer that we concentrate most of our resources on gathering "natural history" data with better tools, such as the photographic devices used by Hershenson, Haith, and Salapatek; the conditioning apparatus used at Brown; the polygraphic procedures used by Dayton and Jones, T. Bower, Frances Graham, and our group (Figs. 4 and 7).

WHERE DO WE STAND AS A SCIENTIFIC ENTERPRISE?

In spite of the recent upsurge in the field of research in human infancy, one does not have to look far to find signs of serious trouble. Whether one is dealing with the practical problems of society or the more esoteric concerns of the student or research worker, one finds the field consistently wanting. At the practical level, parents and educators need to know how to structure the environment of each child so as to make likely optimal development of intellectual, linguistic, emotional, social, and motor capacities. The information needed to guide child-rearing practices and governmental programs which feature infant care is almost nonexistent (White 1969). Parents (in this country at least) who want to do their best by their children cannot turn to a cadre of authorities, nor to definitive writings on the subject.

This strange and important deficit at the practical level is paralleled by and a direct function of a similar void in the scientific literature. I have been to many conferences in recent years where practitioners have literally begged academicians for our pearls of wisdom. It is very disconcerting to have to admit that the cupboard is nearly bare, but it is. An exceptional academic figure will volunteer detailed suggestions. Such material must of current necessity ordinarily be either unsupported by data or constitute an improper generalization from an inadequate data base.

In spite of the fact that psychologists have been studying young children since the late nineteenth century, graduate students beginning the study of infancy today are commonly amazed at how little has been accomplished by the field. Students have asked me about studies which trace the development of fundamental factors such as curiosity or receptive language. My comment is invariably that the only topic in early human development where a proper scientific longitudinal inquiry has really begun is in the area of intellectual development in the work of Piaget (1952). For the issue of curiosity, in addition to Piaget, I usually cite a handful of isolated studies such as Berlyne (1958) or, more recently, Charlesworth (1963, 1966). For receptive language, I suggest McCarthy's review chapter in Carmichael (1960) and the current work of Friedlander et al. (1965). In neither case can I declare that we have done more than scratch the surface of the problem. When a student asks where he may find literature on experimental studies of the role of experience in infancy, I am again obliged to reply that none of Piaget's work in infancy addressed the issue of the role of experience experimentally, and aside from Piaget there are only a handful of people who have ever performed such work (see Chapter 3). The field has simply not dealt with the problem.

Further proof of this can be found by pursuing the literature. There are no definitive treatises on infant behavioral development. Carmichael's manual (1960), an extraordinarily useful book in general, has a chapter on the neonate, which deals mainly with the first week of life. After that one searches in vain for comparable information on the two month to two year period. Peiper's encyclopedic work (1963) provides a very impressive array of factual data on infancy, but the material is neither comprehensive nor integrated. Gesell's work while valuable doesn't fill this need either for reasons mentioned earlier (Gesell and Amatruda 1941). Recently one or two collections of readings on infancy have appeared (Brackbill 1962; Brackbill and Thompson 1967), but these books should more properly be labeled "studies of conditioning processes utilizing a new type of subject" rather than "studies of infancy." In these volumes, one learns how, with great effort, ingenious experimenters have influenced the behavior of infants for brief periods of time, but the reader comes away neither knowing appreciably more about infants, nor convinced that what has been described is relevant to how infants acquire new behaviors. In truth, the authors of such articles rarely have extensive knowledge of infancy beyond the narrow confines of their experimental situations.

The most appropriate word I can think of to describe our progress toward our professional goals during the last 70 years is "pitiful." It is my view that we are appallingly ignorant of (1) the course of development of most major abilities of infants, (2) individual differences in patterns of infant behavior, (3) the interests of infants, (4) the range of environmental circumstances which surround infants, and (5) the laws of development. In other words, we have little scientific knowledge of what infants are like, what their worlds are like, or how environmental circumstances and resultant experiences affect the development of an infant's abilities. We have no available ethology of infancy. We have no natural history exhibits on the human infant and his surround. Perhaps when you've seen one English sparrow, his parents, and their nest, you've seen all there is to see; but, infants take longer to develop, they come in a wider variety, and their rearing circumstances and early experiences are terribly diverse.

Rita Eisenberg, in a recent report (1966), concludes that the field of research on the development of the auditory capacity in human infants is "a vast wasteland." Until my colleagues and I reported our preliminary findings on visual accommodation (Haynes, White, and Held, 1965) there was no information available on whether infants could focus a clear image of a target. The only extensive work, to this day, on the emergence and early development of goal-seeking behavior, curiosity, object permanence, temporal awareness, and other intellectual abilities is that of Piaget on his own children. The only experimental work on the acquisition of language consists of a half dozen small scale unreplicated attempts such as the work of Rheingold on conditioning vocalizations (1961). The only work on auditory preferences of infants is that of Friedlander, McCarthy, and Soforenko (1965) with an *n* of 2 or 3 and a very liimted coverage of age. The only sophisticated data on the emergence of grammatical skills of infants is that of Brown and Bellugi (1964) with an *n* of 3. I could go on.

For those who would study conditioning, there are no dependable compilations of response repertoires for various stages of infancy. Further, since pain, thirst, and starvation are not feasible motivators in human infant work, conditioners need to know what interests infants of various ages. No such data exist. My point is that this is no way to build a science. We cannot continue indefinitely performing grand theoretical analyses and superficially scientific exercises in establishing isolated minutiae.

What then is the current state of development of the field? I have tried to describe an extremely primitive body of scientific knowledge. What we do *not* know is so fundamental and so widespread that the intelligent lay person, for example, often is inclined to believe we're hiding something from him.

But, one cannot bemoan the primitivity of a field indefinitely. In fact, one isn't tempted to at all ordinarily. I have done so, partly because a candid overview of the field should be available and has not been, and partly because I believe the field has been achieving far less than it should. If we are to get our job done, and it is a vital task, I believe we must drastically alter the kind of research effort currently in process.

SOURCES OF DIFFICULTY FOR THE FIELD AND RECOMMENDATIONS FOR CHANGE

Why is it that these basic studies have not been performed? First of all, until recently, children under six years of age were not easily attainable as subjects. (For the period five days to two and a half years, they still are hard to come by.) More significant, however, and more easily correctable are factors inherent in the nature of our profession. Most professional students of child development can be described as part-time experimentalists intent on testing or resolving disputes between theories. We can be described as part-time because, except for an occasional postdoctoral research fellow, the majority of us hold academic positions. Teaching, administrative chores, and professional duties not only reduce the time available for research, but also restrict it to certain hours of the day. We are experimentalists because otherwise we would not be taken very seriously by our colleagues. Clinical reports, anecdotal tidbits, and sweeping theoretical statements, though not uncommon, are looked upon with less and less enthusiasm by serious workers in this field. Further, nonexperimental output is less likely to get published in journals of the American Psychological Association. Finally, we may be said to be preoccupied with theory because most published articles presuppose or state some theoretical position and contain one or more hypotheses which have been deduced from it. Again, such a format is not the one most likely to succeed. Although, understandable, this state of affairs does not, in my opinion, bode well for the field.

Who have been the outstanding men in child development? I count only two, Freud and Piaget. Is it a coincidence that both came from the biological sciences? I don't think so. Neither do I believe it coincidental that the work of both men rests on enormous amounts of nonexperimental, unbiased observation (admittedly, Freud's observations were not of infants). Both Freud and Piaget collected vast quantities of information from subjects under naturalistic or near-naturalistic conditions. Their observations were, of course, guided by theories, but the gap between theory and behavior was very great. The work of these men has a quality of authenticity which suggests that replications will generally be successful, as indeed they have been. The same thing is true about the work of other people who have gathered first-rate observational evidence. When Wolff published his paper on observations of the human neonate (1959), it proved immediately useful and replicable. And, moving to a related field, would anyone doubt the reliability of the descriptions of other species by Lorenz (1952)?

Work of this kind is rare and expensive. The book *Personality in Young Children* by Lois Murphy (1956) describes the development of personality in one child over a three-year period. Several people made major investments of their time to produce this unique chronicle of normal child development. It is a gold mine for students of personality; nowhere else in the literature can one get so close to skillfully collected raw material.

These kinds of studies are powerful. I believe the major reason they are powerful is that child development is a field hungry for facts or, as Wright put it, a field without a natural history (1960), though Wright doesn't make as much of this point as I think he should. We are constantly searching for some material to plug our theories into. Perhaps the most striking example of this condition of much theory and few facts is in developmental psycholinguistics, where the only raw material sufficiently detailed for the purpose of supporting sophisticated theory is that of Roger Brown and Ursula Bellugi (1964). Brown and Bellugi have made the investment of extensive, first-rate observations with three children over many months, and this is all the direct detailed evidence we have.[3] Yet note the importance of the problem, and consider the amount of theorizing that is being generated on the acquisition of language.

It seems to me that child development is overladen with theories and concepts. And, worst of all, these heuristic devices have—with one exception, Gesell's concept of reciprocal interweaving—been imported from foreign soil; psychoanalysis came from studies of middle-class, neurotic Viennese women; sensorimotor theory from studies of mollusks; learning theory from dogs, mice, cats, and monkeys; Gestalt theory from human adults, chimpanzees, and mice; and instinct theory from birds, fish, and

---

[3] It should also be pointed out that their observations began when their subjects were 18 months of age. Few investigators would deny the likely importance for the acquisition of language of experiences between birth and 18 months.

insects. And here is a clue to our dilemma. The data of the behavioral sciences involve interrelations among groups of laws such as those of physics, chemistry, electricity, and experience. The degree of complexity is apparently far beyond that dealt with by the older sciences, yet we devote next to none of our energy to familiarizing ourselves with our subject matter, and we use second-hand theories. In his delightful book, Schaller (1964) decries the fact that so few have studied the gorilla, one of man's closest kin among other animals. Ironically enough, we don't really know much more about children, despite the fact that they are all around us.

It is often remarked that a comprehensive developmental theory is much needed. Actually I agree, but I do not believe we have the raw material out of which to construct a developmental theory of consequence at this time. I think we had better invest most of our resources in sharpening our observational tools and collecting twenty years of solid natural history first.

7

EPILOGUE

A MEMO TO GRADUATE STUDENTS IN
DEVELOPMENTAL PSYCHOLOGY

I FEEL OBLIGED TO WRITE THIS MEMO because I have found this field of research in infancy confused and confusing, frustrating and exciting. I don't believe there is a more important scientific problem than understanding the phenomena and causal processes of human development. The prospect of some day being able to structure the early experiences of each child so as to maximize his prospects for contributing to and enjoying life is of singular importance. You will not, however, find your course as a developmental psychologist clearly laid out. A large number of different types of professionals are concerned with this problem, and few give ringing endorsements to the activities of many of their colleagues. Not only are there child welfare people, educators, pediatricians, psychiatrists, and sociologists on the scene, but, in addition, there are several types of developmental psychologists.

In this book I have described a scientific field in its early developmental stages. From the preceding remarks, it is clear that the field is not only young but also very highly valued by society. In addition, there is the fact of complexity. As a scientific problem, the study of infant development is clearly most resistant to easy solution. Add all these factors and it is virtually inevitable that the field will be characterized by fundamental differences of opinion as to how to generate new knowledge.

Two central features of my teaching are therefore considerations of epistemology and philosophy of science. I strongly advocate philosophy department courses in these topics for every student of developmental psychology. Correspondingly, I advocate a skeptical attitude toward authoritative statements about both content and method in this field. Aside from Piaget, there are few of us who can point with pride to a record of accomplishment in research in infancy to support strong positions. It will not be easy to resist the withering stares of passionate devotees of the *only* "scientifically valid" or the *only* "comprehensive and logical" approach to the field (including those of this writer). Nor will it be easy to cope with severe criticisms and negative judgments from the study sections of funding agencies, which are routinely manned by adherents of one or another extreme position, especially when their decisions will make a big difference to a budding career. Nonetheless, the cause is clearly worth the effort in my opinion. Think of the issues yet to be explored: the emergence and development of curiosity, linguistic ability, cognitive ability, attachment tendencies, and many others. If this sounds like a rather inclusive array, it should, because infancy is both that developmental period where so much of the substrata of human function appear to undergo critical development and also a period in human development which has to this day barely been touched by scientific inquiry.

A MEMO TO AGENCIES WHICH FUND RESEARCH

I believe that a profound change in the policies of funding agencies is necessary. The current demand for information as to how to guide the development of human infants is unprecedented. This demand, being made by a society very concerned about infant and early child development, can only be met currently with the feeblest of recommendations from the custodians of knowledge about early human development. It is my opinion that, considering the resources that have been invested in generating such knowledge over the last thirty years, we have achieved very little. I will not go into a lengthy recitation of what we don't know about infant behavior or about the role of experience in early development (for details see White, in press, and LaCrosse et al., in press), but I believe a clear majority of experienced professionals, especially those responsible for rearing infants, agrees with my view that our overall patterns of research effort and achieved knowledge do not reflect intelligent planning or even very good sense. Rather than grieve about the situation, I would prefer to make some recommendations for improvement.

I believe there is a primary cause for our current stunted development as a field, and I think I know what that obstacle is. While it is unlikely that any single factor is solely to blame for the situation, one seems to be central. The nature of the scientific effort of psychologists studying infants has been and is currently largely shaped by the funding policies of the National Institute of Mental Health, the National Institute of Child Health and Human Development, and, to a lesser extent, by the Office of Education and what used to be the Children's Bureau. In turn, these policies are guided with a very firm hand by the respective independent scientific review groups or study sections. From what I have been able to gather, these few groups are often strongly guided and occasionally dominated by their more persuasive members as is the case in any such group activity. And here is where ultimate responsibility for the disposition of resources and, indirectly, the record of accomplishment must rest. The number of individuals involved is actually very small, probably numbering no more than two dozen. These study section people work very hard, are unquestionably able, and have usually been picked from our own ranks. In spite of all this, it is my view that their efforts have not resulted in anywhere near the achievement record the field is capable of. In fact, by any reasonable standards, I would say the field and they do not deserve passing grades. If this is so, then we must ask why.

I believe the answer lies in the comparative youth of our science and the awesome complexity of the problem of understanding human development. These factors combined with the urgency of society's needs have, I believe, produced a polarization of positions by a small number of key personnel on review panels. This polarization has in turn resulted in rigid review procedures which alternate approval between projects which seem methodologically impeccable or safe but have a topic that is clearly of very low priority, and projects where the importance of the problem is clear but where the methodology is so bad as to guarantee the failure of the inquiry. I have been told many a horror story by first-hand witnesses and participants of how a proposal, if not *totally* unassailable on methodological grounds, is routinely rejected, often to be replaced by an elegant treatment of a topic few believe is worth the effort and expense. On the other hand, there apparently are cases where antiscientific evaluation prevails as a reaction to the aforementioned practice of extreme emphasis on precise measurement, etc. In other instances, there are cases where the issues within the area of inquiry of the agency are dealt with by people without the relevant professional background or a genuine concern. The result is often an unsympathetic and unknowing hearing. One might argue that this argument applies only to exceptional instances and, in any case, is based on inadequate information; perhaps so. Nonetheless, two points argue for the serious consideration of these remarks: (1) Many respected investigators in the profession believe the situation is generally as bad as I have described it and furthermore have time and again been denied research support largely on such inappropriate grounds, and (2) the sorry record of the field as a whole warrants an inquiry.

What can be done? After all the federal government can only turn to the professionals in any field for guidance, and this it has done. What more is possible? I would point out that in turning to professionals in a field as diverse and as fraught with fundamental disagreements as ours, it behooves the federal government and any other funding agency to make certain that it does not foster a concentration of power into the hands of a nonrepresentative few. I believe the study sections and advisory councils for research in developmental psychology and early education should not only be made representative (even at the risk of complicating the decision-making process) but most importantly, they should also regularly include authorities on the philosophy of science. Our field does not seem as yet to know where it's going or how to get there. Why hand the reins over to one or two minority groups when they do not enjoy the confidence of the profession as a whole, when there isn't a history of accomplishment to support their views, and when the field is characterized by fractionation and serious differences of opinion on fundamental principles of procedure? Doesn't it make sense to treat the field as a precious fledgling and provide peacekeepers and qualified advisors who can help guide it to maturity?

The research on early intellectual development performed by Jean Piaget, the Swiss genetic epistemologist, has received considerably more world-wide approbation than that of anyone else in the field. Indeed, it would appear to be in a class by itself. If Piaget's work had depended upon the funding policies currently in vogue, it is quite unlikely that it would ever have begun.

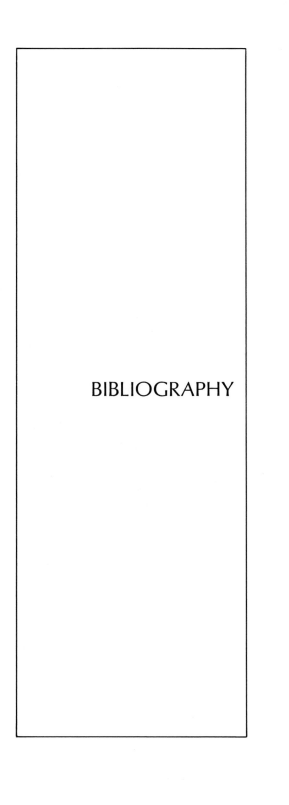

BIBLIOGRAPHY

ABRAHAM, K. Contributions to the theory of the oral character. In *Selected papers.* London: Hogarth Press, 1949, pp. 370-92 (1921).

AHRENS, R. Beitrag zur Entwicklung des Physiognomic-und Memikerkennens. *Zeitschr. Exper. Angew. Psychol.,* 1955, 2, 413-54, 599-633.

AINSWORTH, M. D. SALTER, and BELL, S. M. Some contemporary patterns of mother-infant interaction in the feeding situation. Paper read at the inaugural meeting of the Centre for Advanced Study in the Developmental Sciences and joint study group with the Ciba Foundation, London, Nov. 13-17, 1967.

AMBROSE, J. A. The development of the smiling response in early infancy. In Foss, B. M. (Ed.), *Determinants of infant behavior.* New York: John Wiley & Sons, Inc., 1961, Vol. I, 179-201.

————. The concept of a critical period for the development of social responsiveness in early human infancy. In Foss, B. M. (Ed.), *Determinants of infant behavior.* New York: John Wiley & Sons, Inc., 1963, Vol. II, 201-25.

ANDERSON, L. D. The predictive value of infancy tests in relation to intelligence at five years. *Child Development,* 1939, 10, 203-12 [21-23].

BARTOSHUK, A. K. Human neonatal cardiac acceleration to sound: habituation and dishabituation. *Percept. Mot. Skills,* 1962, 15, 15-27.

BAYLEY, N. Mental growth in young children. *Yearb. Nat. Soc. Stud. Educ.,* 1940, 39, Vol. II, 11-47 [21-22, 314].

————. Comparisons of mental and motor test scores for ages 1-15 months by sex, birth order, race, geographical location, and education of parents. *Child Development,* 1965, 36, 379-411.

BERLYNE, D. The influence of the albedo and complexity of stimuli on visual fixation in the human infant. *Brit. J. Psychol.,* 1958, 49, 315-18.

BIJOU, S. W.   Ages, stages, and the naturalization of human development. *Amer. Psychologist,* June 1968, *23,* 6.

BIRNS, B.   Individual differences in human neonates responses to stimulation. *Child Development,* March 1965, *36,* No. 1.

BIRNS, B., BLAND, M., and BRIDGER, W. H.   The effectiveness of various soothing techniques on human neonates. *Psycho. Med.,* July-Aug. 1966, *28,* No. 4, Part 1.

BITTERMAN, M. E.   Electromyographic recording of eyelid movements. *Amer. J. Psychol.,* 1945, *58,* 112.

BLOOM, S. B.   *Stability and change in human characteristics.* New York: John Wiley & Sons, Inc., 1965.

BOWER, T. G. R.   Discrimination of depth in pre-motor infants. *Psychon. Sci.,* 1964, Vol. I, 368.

————.   Slant perception and shape constancy in infants. *Science,* Feb. 18, 1966.

BOWLBY, J.   *Maternal care and mental health.* Geneva: World Health Organization, Monograph 2, 1951.

————.   The nature of the child's tie to his mother. *Int. J. Psychoanal.,* 1958, *39,* 350-73.

BRACKBILL, Y.   Research and clinical work with children. In *Some Views on Soviet Psychology.* American Psychological Association, Inc., 1962, Chap. 5.

BRACKBILL, Y., and THOMPSON, G. G.   *Behavior in infancy and early childhood.* New York: Free Press of Glencoe, Inc., 1967.

BRIDGES, K. M. B.   Emotional development in early infancy. *Child Development,* 1932, *3,* 324-34.

BRODY, S.   *Patterns of mothering.* New York: International Universities Press, 1951.

BROWN, R., and BELLUGI, U.   Three processes in the child's acquisition of syntax. *Harvard Educ. Rev.,* 1964, *34,* 133-51.

BUHLER, C., and HETZER, H.   *The first year of life.* New York: John Day, 1930.

————.   *Testing children's development from birth to school age.* New York: Farrar & Reinhart, 1935.

CALDWELL, B. M.   The effects of infant care. In Hoffman, M. L., and Hoffman, L. W. (Eds.), *Review of Child Development Research.* New York: Russell Sage Foundation, 1964, Vol. I, 9-87.

CALDWELL, B. M., et al.   Mother-infant interaction in monomatric and polymatric families. *Amer. J. Orthopsychiat.,* 1963, *33,* 653-64.

CALDWELL, B. M., WRIGHT, C. M., HONIG, A. S., and TANNENBAUM, J.   Infant day care and attachment. Paper read as part of a panel on "Impact of Evolving Institutional Settings on Early Child Development: Issues and Research Findings" at the 46th Annual Meeting of the American Orthopsychiatric Assoc., April 1969.

CAMPBELL, D.   Activity in new-borns the first week of life. Paper read at the biennial meeting of the SRCD, New York City, April 1967.

CARMICHAEL, L.   *Manual of child psychology* (2nd ed.). New York: John Wiley & Sons, Inc., 1960.

CASLER, L.   The effects of extra tactile stimulation on a group of institutionalized infants. *Gen. Psychol. Monograph,* 1965, *71,* 137-75.

————.   Maternal deprivation: a critical review of the literature. *Monograph SRCD,* 1961, *26,* 1-64.

CATTELL, PSYCHE. *The measurement of intelligence of infants and young children.* New York: Psychological Corporation, 1940.

CHARLESWORTH, W. R. The role of surprise or novelty in the motivation of curiosity behavior. Paper read at SRCD, Berkeley, April 1963.

————. Persistence of orienting and attending behavior in infants as a function of stimulus-locus uncertainty. *Child Development,* 1966, 37, 473-90.

CHURCH, J. *Three babies: biographies of cognitive development.* New York: Random House, Inc., 1966.

COLE, L. *A history of education.* New York: Rinehart & Company, 1959.

CROWELL, D. H., DAVIS, C. M., CHUN, B. J., and SPELLACY, F. J. The galvanic skin reflex in human neonates. Unpublished manuscript, Newborn Psychological Research Laboratory, Pacific Biomedical Research Center, Univ. of Hawaii, Honolulu, March 1965.

DARWIN, C. *The descent of man.* Modern Library, 1871.

DAVID, M., and APPEL, G. A study of nursery care and nurse-infant interaction. In Foss, B. M. (Ed.), *Determinants of infant behavior.* New York: John Wiley & Sons, Inc., 1961, pp. 121-36.

DAYTON, G. O., and JONES, M. H. Analysis of characteristics of fixation and reflex in infants by use of direct current electroculography. *Neurology,* 1964, pp. 1151-56.

DAYTON, G. O., JONES, M. H., AIU, P., RAWSON, R. A., STEELE, B., and ROSE, M. Developmental study of coordinated eye movements in the human infant. II. An electro-oculographic study of the fixation reflex in the newborn. *Archives of Ophthalmology,* 1964, 71, 871-75.

DECARIE, T. G. *Intelligence and affectivity in early childhood.* New York: International Universities Press, Inc., 1965.

DENENBERG, B. H., and KARAS, G. G. Effects of differential infantile handling upon weight gain and mortality in the rat and mouse. *Science,* 1959, 130, 629-30.

DENENBERG, V. H. Stimulation in infancy, emotional reactivity, and exploratory behavior. In Glass, D. H. (Ed.), *Biology and behavior neurophysiology and emotion.* New York: Russell Sage Foundation and Rockefeller University Press, 1967.

DENNIS, W., and DENNIS, M. G. The effect of cradling practices upon the onset of walking in Hopi children. *J. Genet. Psychol.,* 1940, 56, 77-86.

DENNIS, W., and DENNIS, S. G. Infant development under conditions of restricted practice and minimum social stimulations. *Genet. Psychol. Monographs,* 1941, 23, 147, 149-55.

DENNIS, W., and NAJARIAN, P. Infant development under environmental handicap. *Psychol. Monograph,* 1957, 71, No. 7.

DENNIS, W., and SAYEGH, Y. The effect of supplementary experiences upon the behavioral development of infants in institutions. *Child Development,* March 1965, 36, No. 1.

DUKE-ELDER, W. S. *Textbook of ophthalmology,* Vol. IV. St. Louis: The C. V. Mosby Co., 1949.

EIBL-EIBESFELDT, I. Concepts of ethology and their significance in the study of human behavior. In Stevenson, H. W., Hess, E. H., and Rheingold, H. C. (Eds.), *Early behavior: Comparative and developmental approaches.* New York: John Wiley & Sons, Inc., 1967, pp. 127-47.

EISENBERG, R. B. The development of hearing in man: An assessment of current status. Report to the National Advisory Neurological Disease and Blindness Council, Sept. 7, 1966.

————. Auditory behavior in the human neonate: Functional properties of sound and their ontogenetic implications. *International Audiology—Audiologie Internationale,* Feb. 1969, 8, No. 1, 34-45.

ENGEN, T., and LIPSITT, L. P. Decrement and recovery of responses to olfactory stimuli in the human neonate. *J. Comp. Physiol. Psychol.,* 1965, 59, 312-16.

ERICKSON, E. H. *Childhood and society.* New York: W. W. Norton & Company, Inc., 1950.

ESCALONA, S. K. Emotional development in the first year of life. In Senn, Milton J. E. (Ed.), *Problems of infancy and childhood.* New York: Josiah Macy Jr. Foundation, 1953, pp. 11-92.

————. The study of individual differences and the problem of state. *J. Amer. Acad. Child Psychiatry,* 1962, 1, 11-37.

ESCALONA, S. K., and CORMAN, H. Albert Einstein scales of sensori-motor development. Yeshiva University, 1968 (ditto report).

ESCALONA, S. K., and HEIDER, G. M. *Prediction and outcome.* New York: Basic Books, Inc., Publishers, 1959.

ESCALONA, S. K., and LEITCH, M. Early phases of personality development. A non-normative study of infant behavior. *Monograph Soc. Res. Child Development,* 1952, 17, No. 1.

FANTZ, R. L. Pattern vision in newborn infants. *Science,* 1963, 140, 296-97.

————. A method for studying depth perception in infants under six months of age. *Psychol. Rec.,* 1961a, 11, 27-32.

————. Pattern vision in young infants. *Scientific American,* 1961b, 204, 66-72.

————. Visual experience in infants: decreased attention to familiar patterns relative to novel ones. *Science,* 1964, 146, 668-70.

FANTZ, R. L., and NEVIS, S. The predictive value of changes in visual preferences in early infancy. In Hellmuth, J. (Ed.), *The exceptional infant,* Vol. I. Seattle, Wash.: Special Child Publications, 1967.

FANTZ, R. L., ORDY, J. M., and UDELF, M. S. Maturation of pattern vision in infants during the first six months. *J. of Comp. Physiol. Psychol.,* 1962, 55, No. 6, 907-17.

FELDMAN, W. M. *Principles of ante-natal and post-natal child physiology, pure and applied.* London: Longmans, Green & Co., 1920.

FERENCZI, S. Stages in the development of the sense of reality. In Van Teslaar, J. S. (Ed.), *An outline of psychoanalysis.* New York: Boni and Liveright, 1924.

FERGUSON, G. A. *Statistical analysis in psychology and education.* New York: McGraw-Hill Book Company, 1959.

FITZGERALD, H. E., LINTZ, L. M., BRACKBILL, Y., and ADAMS, G. Time perception and conditioning and autonomic response in human infants. *Percept. Mot. Skills,* 1967, 24, 479-86.

FLAVELL, J. *The developmental psychology of Jean Piaget.* Princeton, N.J.: D. Van Nostrand Co., Inc., 1963.

FREUD, S. Three essays on the theory of sexuality (1905). *Standard edition of complete psychological works of Sigmund Freud,* Vol. 7, 1901–1905. London: Hogarth Press & Institute of Psychoanalysis, 1957.

FRIEDLANDER, B. Z., McCARTHY, J. J., and SOFORENKO, A. Z. Automated psychological evaluation and stimulus enrichment with severely retarded institutionalized infants. Paper read at American Association on Mental Deficiency (Psychology Section), June 1965.

FRIES, M. E., and WOOLF, P. J. Some hypotheses on the role of the congenital activity type in personality development. *Psychoanal. Study of the Child,* 1953, *8,* 48-62.

FURFEY, P. H., and MUEHLENBEIN, J. The validity of infant intelligence tests. *J. Genet. Psychol.,* 1932, *40,* 219-23 [21-23].

GESELL, A., and AMATRUDA, C. S. *Developmental diagnosis.* New York: Hoeber, 1941.

GESELL, A., and ILG, F. *Infant and child in the culture of today.* New York and London: Harper & Row, Publishers, 1943.

GESELL, A., ILG, F., and BULLIS, G. F. *Vision: its development in infant and child.* New York: Hoeber, 1949.

GEWIRTZ, J. L. On the choice of relevant variables and levels of conceptual analysis in environment-infant interaction research. Presented at the Merrill-Palmer Institute Conference on Research and Teaching of Infant Development, Feb. 15-17, 1968. *Merrill-Palmer Quart.* (in press).

GEWIRTZ, J. L., and GEWIRTZ, H. B. Stimulus conditions, infant behaviors, and social learning in four Israeli child-rearing environments. In Foss, B. M. (Ed.), *Determinants of infant behavior,* Vol. III. New York: Wiley & Sons, Inc., 1965.

GIBSON, E. J., and WALK, R. D. The visual cliff. *Scientific American,* 1960, *202,* 64-71.

GOLLIN, E. S. Research trends in infant learning. In Hellmuth, J. (Ed.), *Exceptional infant.* Seattle, Washington: Special Child Publications, 1967.

GORDON, I. J., et al. Reaching the child through parent education. The Institute for Development of Human Resources, Univ. of Florida, Gainesville, Florida, Feb. 1969.

GORMAN, J. J., COGAN, D. G., and GELLIS, S. S. An apparatus for grading the visual acuity of infants on the basis of optokinetic nystagmus. *Pediatrics,* 1957, *19,* 1088-92.

GRAHAM, F. K., and CLIFTON, R. K. Heart rate change as a component of the orienting response. *Psychol. Bull.,* 1966, *4,* 185-86.

GRANIT, R. *The sensory mechanisms of the retina.* London: Oxford University Press, 1947.

GRAY, P. H. Theory and evidence of imprinting in human infants. *J. Psychol.,* 1958, *46,* 155-56.

GREENBERG, D., UZGIRIS, I. C., and McV. HUNT, J. Hastening the development of blink-response with looking. *J. Genet. Psychol.,* 1968, *113,* 167-76.

GRIFFITHS, R. *The abilities of babies.* London: University of London Press, 1954.

HALVERSON, H. M. An experimental study of prehension in infants by means of systematic cinema records. *Genet. Psychol. Monograph,* 1932, *10,* 110-286.

HARLOW, H. F. Development of affection in primates. In Bliss, E. L. (Ed.), *Roots of behavior.* New York: Harper & Row, Publishers, 1962.

HARTLINE, H. K. Inhibition of activity of visual receptors by illuminating nearby retinal areas in the limulus eye. *Fed. Proc.,* 1949, *8,* 69.

HAYNES, H. M.   Clinical observations with dynamic retinoscopy. *Optometric Weekly,* 1960, *51,* 2243-46.

HAYNES, H., WHITE, B. L., and HELD, R. M.   Visual accommodation in human infants. *Science, 1965, 148,* 528-30.

HEBB, D. O.   *A neuropsychological theory.* New York: John Wiley & Sons, Inc., 1949.

HELD, R. M.   Exposure-history as a factor in maintaining stability of perception and co-ordination. *J. Nerv. Ment. Dis.,* 1961, *132,* 26-32.

HELD, R., and BOSSOM, J.   Neonatal deprivation and adult rearrangement: complementary techniques for analyzing plastic sensory-motor coordinations. *J. Comp. Physiol. Psychol.,* 1961, *54,* 33-37.

HELD, R., and HEIN, A.   Adaptation of disarranged hand-eye coordinations contingent upon reafferent stimulation. *Percept. Motor Skills,* 1958, *8,* 87-90.

————.   Movement-produced stimulation in the development of visually-guided behavior. *J. Comp. Physiol. Psychol.,* 1963, *56,* 872-76.

HELD, R., and SCHLANK, M.   Adaptation to optically-increased distance of the hand from the eye by reafferent stimulation. *American J. Psychol.,* 1959, *72,* 603-5.

HERSHENSON, M.   Visual discrimination in the human newborn. *J. Comp. Physiol. Psychol.,* 1964, *58,* 270-76.

HERSHENSON, M., MUNSINGER, H., and KESSEN, W.   Preference for shapes of intermediate variability in the newborn human. *Science, 1965, 147,* 630-31.

HINDE, R. A.   The behavior of the Great Tit (Parnsmajer) and some other related species. *Behavior,* 1952, Supp. No. 2, pp. 1-201.

————.   *Animal behaviour.* New York: McGraw-Hill Book Company, 1966.

HOROWITZ, F. D.   Infant learning and development: Retrospect and prospect. *Merrill-Palmer Quart. Behav. Development,* 1968, *14,* 101-20.

HUBEL, D. H., and WIESEL, T. N.   Receptive fields, binocular interaction and functional architecture in the cat's visual cortex. *J. Physiol.,* 1962, *160,* 106-54.

HUNT, J. McV.   *Intelligence and experience.* New York: The Ronald Press Company, 1961.

————.   Intrinsic motivation and its role in psychological development. In Levine, David (Ed.), *Nebraska Symposium on Motivation.* Lincoln, Nebraska: University of Nebraska Press, 1965, pp. 189-282.

IRWIN, O. C.   The amount and nature of activities of newborn infants under constant external stimulating conditions during the first ten days of life. *Genet. Psychol. Monographs,* 1930, *8,* 1-92.

————.   The amount of motility of seventy-three newborn infants. *J. Comp. Psychol.,* 1932a, *14,* 415-28.

————.   Infant speech: effect of systematic reading of stories. *J. Speech Hear. Res.,* 1960, *3,* 187-90.

JENSEN, A. R.   How much can we boost IQ and scholastic achievement? *Harvard Educ. Rev.* Montpelier, Vermont: Capital City Press, 1969, *39,* No. 1.

JONES, F. W.   *Arboreal man.* London: Edward Arnold (Publishers) Ltd., 1916.

KAGAN, J.   American longitudinal research on psychological development. *Child Development,* 1964, *35,* 1-32.

KAYE, H.   The conditioned Babkin reflex in human newborns. *Psychon. Sci.*, 1965, 2, 287-88.

KNOBLOCH, H., and PASAMANICK, B.   Environmental factors affecting human development, before and after birth. *Pediatrics*, August 1960, 26, No. 2.

KOOPMAN, P. R., and AMES, E. W.   Infant's preferences for facial arrangements: a failure to replicate. Paper read at meetings of the SRCD, New York City, March 1967.

KORNER, A. F., and GROBSTEIN, R.   Visual alertness as related to soothing in neonates: implications for maternal stimulation and early deprivation. *Child Development*, Dec. 1966, 37, No. 4.

KUFFLER, S. W., FITZHUGH, R., and BARLOW, H. B.   Maintained activity in the cat's retina in light and darkness. *J. Gen. Physiol.*, 1957, 40, 683-702.

LACROSSE, E. R., LEE, P. C., LITMAN, F., OGILVIE, D. M., STODOLSKY, S. S., and WHITE, B. L.   The first six years of life: a report on current research and educational practice. *Gen. Psychol. Monograph* (in press).

LEWIS, M. M.   *Infant speech.* New York: The Humanities Press, Inc., 1951.

————.   *How children learn to speak.* New York: Basic Books, 1959.

————.   *Language thought and personality in infancy and childhood.* New York: Basic Books, 1963.

LEWIS, M., GOLDBERG, S., and RAUSCH, M.   Attention distribution as a function of novelty and familiarity. *Psychon. Sci.*, 1967, 7 (6).

LETTVIN, J. Y., MATURANA, H. R., McCULLOCH, W. S., and PITTS, W. H.   What the frog's eye tells the frog's brain. *Proc. Instit. Radio engineers*, 47, 1959, 1940-51.

LEVINE, S.   Infantile experience and resistance to physiological stress. *Science*, 1957, 126-405.

LING, B. C.   A genetic study of sustained visual fixation and associated behavior in the human infant from birth to six months. *J. Genet. Psychol.*, 1942, 61, 227-77.

LINTZ, L. M., and FITZGERALD, H.   Apparatus for eyeblink conditioning in infants. *J. of Exp. Child Psychol.*, 1966, 4, 276-79.

LINTZ, L. M., FITZGERALD, H. E., and BRACKBILL, Y.   Conditioning the eyeblink response to sound in infants. *Psychon. Sci.*, 1967, 7 (12).

LIPSITT, L. P.   Learning in the first year of life. In Lipsitt, L. P., and Spiker, C. C. (Eds.). *Advances in child development and behavior*, Vol. I. New York: Academic Press, 1963, 147-95.

————.   Learning in the human infant. In Stevenson, H. W., Hess, E. H., and Rheingold, H. L. (Eds.), *Early behavior: comparative and developmental approaches.* New York: John Wiley & Sons, Inc., 1967, 225-47.

LIPSITT, L. P., PEDERSEN, L. J., and DELUCIA, C.   Conjugate reinforcement of operant responding in infants. *Psychon. Sci.*, 1966, 4, 67-68.

LOCKARD, R. B.   The albino rat: a defensible choice or a bad habit? *J. of Amer. Psychol. Assoc., Inc.*, Oct. 1968, 23, 734-42.

LORENZ, K.   *Evolution and modification of behavior.* Chicago: The University of Chicago Press, 1965.

————.   *King Solomon's ring.* New York: Crowell, Collier and Macmillan, Inc., 1952.

MARQUIS, D. P.   Learning in the neonate: the modification of behavior under three feeding schedules. *J. Exp. Psychol.*, Oct. 1941, 29, No. 4.

MASON, W. A., DAVENPORT, R. K., JR., and MANZEL, E. W., JR.   Early experience and the social development of Rhesus monkeys and chimpanzees. In Newton, G., and Levine, S. (Eds.), *Early experience and behavior*. Springfield, Ill.: Charles C Thomas, Publisher, 1968.

MASON, W. A., and GREEN, P. C.   The effects of social restriction on the behavior of Rhesus monkeys, IV: Responses to a novel environment and to an alien species. *J. Comp. Physiol. Psychol.*, 1962, *55*, 363-68.

McCALL, R. B., and KAGAN, J.   Stimulus-schema discrepancy and attention in the infant. *J. of Experimental Child Psychol.*, 1967, *5*, 381-90.

McCARTHY, D.   Language development in children. In Carmichael, L. (Ed.), *Manual of child psychology* (2nd ed.). New York: John Wiley & Sons, Inc., 1954, pp. 492-630.

McGRAW, M. B.   *The neuromuscular maturation of the human infant*. New York: Hafner Publishing Company, Inc., 1943.

MEIER, G. W.   Infantile experience and resistance to physiological stress. *Science*, 1957, 126-405.

————.   Infantile handling and development in Siamese kittens. *J. Comp. Physiol. Psychol.*, 1961, *54*, 284-86.

MIKAELIAN, H. H., and HELD, R. M.   Two types of adaptation to an optically-routed visual field. *Amer. J. Psychol.*, 1964, *77*, 257-63.

MOLTZ, H.   Imprinting: empirical basis and theoretical significance. *Psychol. Bull.*, 1960, *57*, 291-314.

MORGAN, G. A., and RICCIUTI, H. A.   Infants' responses to strangers during the first year. In Foss, B. M. (Ed.), *Determinants of infant behavior*, Vol. IV. New York: John Wiley & Sons, Inc., 1968.

MOSS, H. A.   Sex, age and state as determinants of mother-infant interactions. *Merrill-Palmer Quart. of Behav. Development*, 1967, *13*, 19-36.

MURPHY, L. B., and ASSOCIATES.   *Personality in young children*, Vol. II. New York: Basic Books, 1956.

NEWTON, G., and LEVINE, S. (Eds.)   *Early experience and behavior*. Springfield, Ill.: Charles C Thomas, Publisher, 1968.

OURTH, L., and BROWN, K. B.   Inadequate mothering and disturbance in the neonatal period. *Child Development*, 1961, *32*, 287-95.

PAINTER, G.   Developing the potential of the culturally disadvantaged infant. Presented at the 46th Annual International Convention of the Council for Exceptional Children, April 14-20, 1968, New York City.

PAPOUSEK, H.   Conditioned motor digestive reflexes in infants. II, a new experimental method for the investigation. *Česk. Pediat.*, 1961, *15*, 981-88.

PAPOUSEK, H., and BERNSTEIN, P.   The function of conditioning stimulation in the human neonate and infants in the functions of stimulation in early post natal development (in press).

PASCAL, J. I.   *Modern retinoscopy*. London: Hatton, 1930.

PEIPER, A.   Cerebral function in infancy and childhood. In Wortis, J. (Ed.), *The international behavioral science series*. New York: Consultants Bureau, 1961.

PIAGET, J.   *The origins of intelligence in children* (2nd ed.). New York: International Universities Press, 1952.

————.   *The construction of reality in the child*. New York: Basic Books, 1954.

POLAK, P. R., EMDE, R. N., and SPITZ, R. A.   The smiling response. II: Visual discrimination and the onset of depth perception. *J. Nerv. Ment. Dis.*, Nov. 1964, *139*, Serial No. 984.

PRATT, K.   The neonate. In Carmichael, L. (Ed.), *Manual of child psychology* (2nd ed.). New York: John Wiley & Sons, Inc., 1954, 215-92.

PRECHTL, H. F. R.   The directed head-turning response and allied movements of the human baby. *Behavior*, 1958, *13*, 212-42.

————.   Problems of behavioral studies in the new-born infant. In Lehrmann, D. S., Hinde, R. A., and Shaw, R. (Eds.), *Advances in the study of behavior.* New York: Academic Press Inc., 1965, *I*, 75-98.

RHEINGOLD, H. L.   The modification of social responsiveness in institutional babies. *Monograph Soc. Res. in Child Development*, 1956, *21*, Serial No. 63, No. 2.

————.   The effects of environmental stimulation upon social and exploratory behavior in the human infant. In Foss, B. M. (Ed.), *Determinants of infant behavior.* New York: John Wiley & Sons, Inc., 1961, *I*, 143-71.

RHEINGOLD, H. L., and BAYLEY, N.   The later effects of an experimental modification of mothering. *Child Development*, 1959, *30*, 363-72.

RHEINGOLD, H. L., GEWIRTZ, J. L., and ROSS, H. W.   Social conditioning of vocalizations in the infant. *J. Comp. Physiol. Psychol.*, Vol. 52, No. 1, Feb., 1959.

RICCIUTI, H. N.   Object grouping and selective ordering behavior in 12- to 24-month-old infants. Paper read at Conference on Infancy Research at Merrill-Palmer Institute, Detroit, Mich., Feb. 1964.

————.   Social and emotional behavior in infancy: some developmental issues and problems. *Merrill-Palmer Quart. of Behav. Development* (in press).

RICCIUTI, H. N., and JOHNSON, L. J.   Developmental changes in categorizing behavior from infancy to the early pre-school years. Paper read at the SRCD Meeting, Minneapolis, Minn., March 1965.

RIESEN, A. H.   Plasticity of behavior: psychological series. In Harlow, H., and Woolsey, C. (Eds.), *Biological and biochemical bases of behavior.* Univ. of Wisconsin Press, 1958, pp. 425-50.

SALAPATEK, P., and KESSEN, W.   Visual scanning of triangles by the human newborn. *J. of Exp. Child Psychol.*, 1966, *3*, 155-67.

SALK, L.   The effects of the normal heartbeat sound on the behavior of the new-born infant: implications for mental health. *World Mental Health*, 1960, *12*.

SCHAEFFER, E. S.   Infant Education Research project, Washington, D. C. Pre-school program in compensatory education I, 1969.

SCHAEFFER, H. R., and EMERSON, P. E.   The developments of social attachments in infancy. Monographs of SRCD, 1964, *29*, (3, Ser. No. 94).

SCHALLER, G.   *The year of the gorilla.* New York: Ballantine Books, Inc., 1964.

SCHWARTING, B. H.   Testing infant's vision. *American J. Ophthal.*, 1954, *38*, 714-15.

SCOTT, J. P.   *Early experience and the organization of behavior.* Belmont, Calif.: Wadsworth, 1968.

SIEGEL, A. E.   Editorial. *Child Development*, 1967, *38*, 4, 901.

SIEGEL, S.   *Nonparametric statistics for the behavioral sciences.* New York: McGraw-Hill Book Company, 1956, pp. 116-27.

SIQUELAND, E.   Operant conditioning of head turning in four-month infants. *Psychon. Sci.,* 1964, Vol. I, 223-24.

SKEELS, H. M.   Adult status of children with contrasting early life experiences. Monographs of SRCD, 1956, *31,* No. 3, Serial No. 105.

SLATAPER, F. J.   Age norms of refraction and vision. *Archives of Ophthalmology,* 1950, *43,* 466-81.

SPELT, D. K.   Conditioned responses in the human fetus in utero. *Psychol. Bull.,* 1938, 35, 712-13.

SPITZ, R. A.   Hospitalism: an inquiry into the genesis of psychiatric conditions in early childhood. In Freud, A., Hartmann, H., and Kris, E. (Eds.), *The Psychoanalytic Study of the Child.* New York: International Universities Press, 1945, Vol. I, 53-74.

————.   *The first year of life: a psychoanalytic study of normal and deviant development of object relations.* New York: International Universities Press, 1965.

SPITZ, R. A., and WOLF, K. M.   The smiling response. *Gen. Psychol. Monograph,* 1946, *34,* 57-125.

STECHLER, G.   Newborn attention as affected by medication during labor. *Science,* 1964, *144,* 315-17.

SULLIVAN, H. S.   *The interpersonal theory of psychiatry.* New York: W. W. Norton & Company, Inc., 1953.

THOMAS, A., CHESS, S., BIRCH, H. G., HERTZIG, M. E., and KORN, S.   *Behavioral individuality in early childhood.* New York: New York Univ. Press, 1963.

THORPE, W. H.   *Learning and instinct in animals.*   London: Methuen & Co. Ltd., 1956.

TINBERGEN, N.   On war and peace in animals and man. *Science,* June 1968, *160,* 1411-18.

TWITCHELL, T. E.   The automatic grasping responses of infants. *Neuropsychologia,* 1965a, *3,* 247-59.

————.   Normal motor development. *J. of the Amer. Physical Therapy Assoc.,* May 1965b, *45,* 5.

UZGIRIS, I. C., and HUNT, J. McV.   An instrument for assessing infant psychological development. Urbana, Ill.: Univ. of Illinois, Feb. 1966. (Unpublished ms.)

WATSON, J. B., and MORGAN, J. J. B.   Emotional reactions and psychological experimentation. *Amer. J. Psychol.,* 1917, *28,* 163-74.

WEIKART, D. P.   Ypsilanti-Carnegie Infant Education Project. Progress Report. Department of Research and Development, Ypsilanti Public Schools, Ypsilanti, Michigan, Sept. 1969.

WEISBERG, P.   Social and nonsocial conditioning of infant vocalizations. *Child Development,* 1963, *34,* 377-88.

WHITE, B. L.   The initial coordination of sensorimotor schemas in human infants—Piaget's ideas and the role of experience. In Flavell, J. H., and Elkind, D. (Eds.), *Studies in cognitive development: essays in honor of Jean Piaget.* New York: Oxford University Press, 1969a, pp. 237-56.

————.   Child development research: an edifice without a foundation. *Merrill-Palmer Quart. of Behav. Development,* 1969b, *15,* No. 1, 50-79.

————.   Moment-to-moment tasks of young children. Paper read at a symposium presented at the SRCD, Santa Monica, Calif., March 26-29, 1969c.

————.   The role of experience in the behavioral development of human infants: current status and recommendation. In Caldwell, B., and Ricciuti, H. (Eds.), *Review of child development research.* New York: Russell Sage Foundation. Vol. III (in press).

————. An experimental approach to the effects of experience on early human behavior. In Hill, J. P. (Ed.), *Minnesota symposium on child psychology.* Minneapolis, Minn.: Univ. of Minnesota Press, 1967, Vol. I, 201-25.

————. Second-order problems in studies of perceptual development. In the Proceedings of a Conference sponsored by the Institute for Juvenile Research, Illinois State Department of Mental Health and National Institute of Child Health and Human Development—National Institutes of Health, 1966, 5-23.

WHITE, B. L., and CASTLE, P. W. Visual exploratory behavior following postnatal handling of human infants. *Perceptual and Motor Skills,* Southern Universities Press, 1964, *18,* 497-502.

WHITE, B. L., CASTLE, P., and HELD, R. Observations on the development of visually-directed reaching. *Child Development,* 1964, *35,* 349-64.

WHITE, B. L., and CLARK, K. R. An apparatus for eliciting and recording the eyeblink. In Ammons, Carroll H. (Ed.), *Psychological Reports—Perceptual and Motor Skills,* 1968, *27,* 959-64.

WHITE, B. L., and HELD, R. Plasticity of sensorimotor development in the human infant. In Rosenblith, J. F., and Allinsmith, W. (Eds), *Causes of behavior: readings in child development and educational psychology* (2nd ed.). Boston, Mass.: Allyn & Bacon, 1966, pp. 60-71.

WHITE, R. W. Motivation reconsidered: the concept of competence. *The Psychol. Rev.,* Sept. 1959, *66,* No. 5.

WICKLEGREN, L. W. Convergence in the human newborn. Paper read at the American Psychological Association, Sept. 1966.

WINER, B. J. *Statistical principles in experimental design.* New York: McGraw-Hill Book Company, 1962.

WOLFF, P. H. The developmental psychologies of Jean Piaget and psychoanalysis. *Psychol. Issues,* 1960, *2,* 1-181.

————. Observations on newborn infants. *Psychosom. Med.,* 1959, *21,* 110-18.

————. Observations on the early development of smiling. In Foss, B. M. (Ed.), *Determinants of infant behavior.* New York: John Wiley & Sons, Inc., 1963, Vol. 2, 113-38.

WOLFF, P. H., and WHITE, B. L. Visual pursuit and attention in young infants. *J. of Child Psychiatry,* 1965, *4,* No. 3.

WRIGHT, H. F. Observational child study. In P. Mussen (Ed.), *Handbook of research methods in child development.* New York: John Wiley & Sons, Inc., 1960, pp. 71-139.

YARROW, L. J. Maternal deprivation: toward an empirical and conceptual re-evaluation. *Psychol. Bull.,* 1961, *58,* 459-90.

————. Separation from parents during early childhood. In Hoffman, M. L., and Hoffman, L. W. (Eds.), *Review of Child Development Research,* Vol. I. New York: Russell Sage Foundation, 1964.

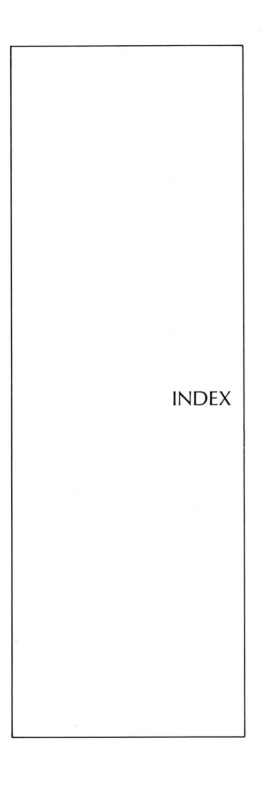

INDEX

DATE DUE